I0715368

USING AUTHORITY,

COMPLEX GEOMETRY

NEW YORK CITY HOUSING AUTHORITY, BROOKLYN.

by Ian Reid

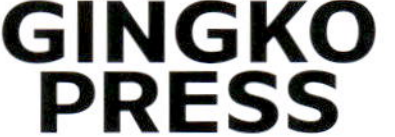

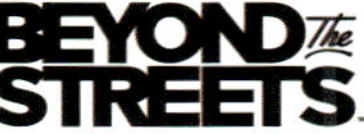

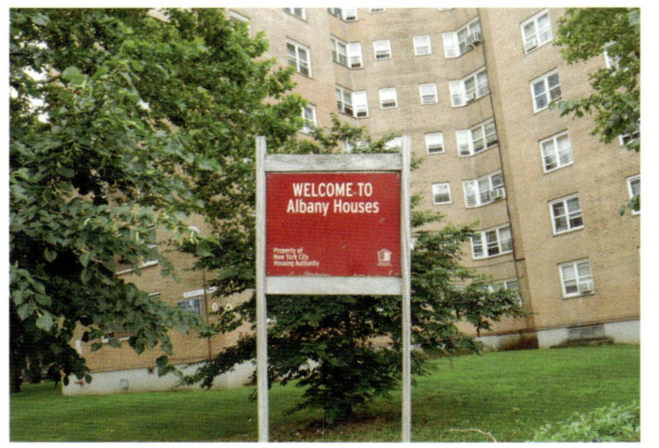
WELCOME TO
Albany Houses
Property of
New York City
Housing Authority

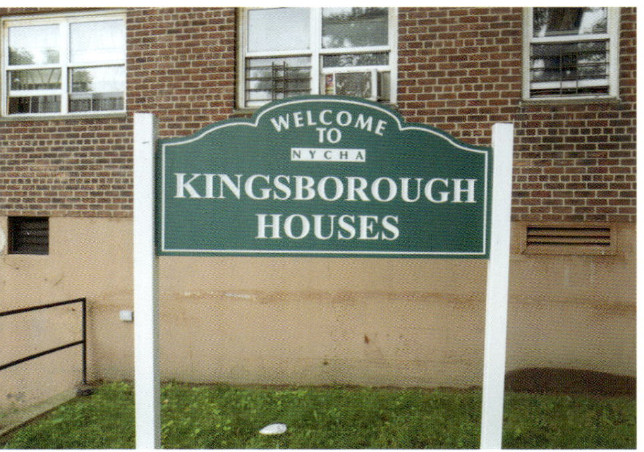
WELCOME
TO
NYCHA
KINGSBOROUGH
HOUSES

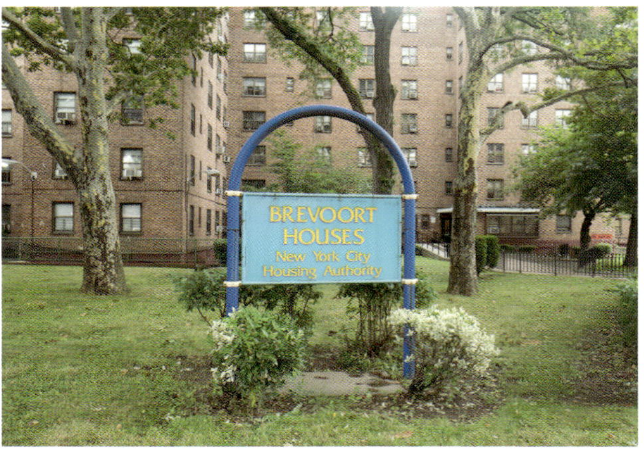
BREVOORT
HOUSES
New York City
Housing Authority

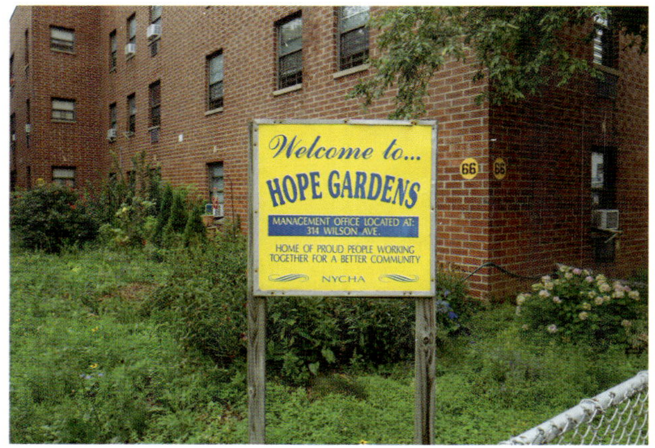
Welcome to...
HOPE GARDENS
MANAGEMENT OFFICE LOCATED AT:
314 WILSON AVE.
HOME OF PROUD PEOPLE WORKING
TOGETHER FOR A BETTER COMMUNITY
NYCHA

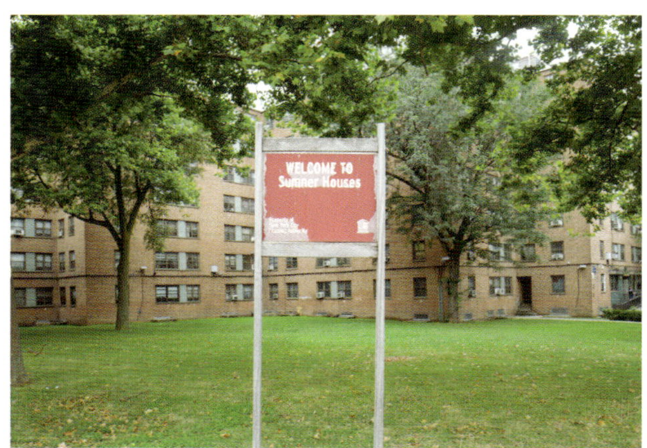
WELCOME TO
Sumner Houses

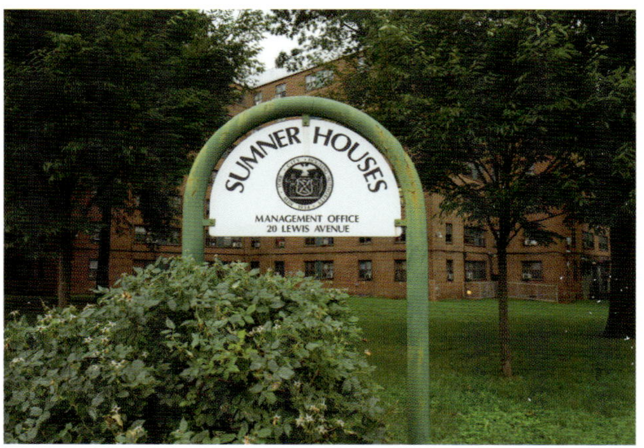
SUMNER HOUSES
MANAGEMENT OFFICE
20 LEWIS AVENUE

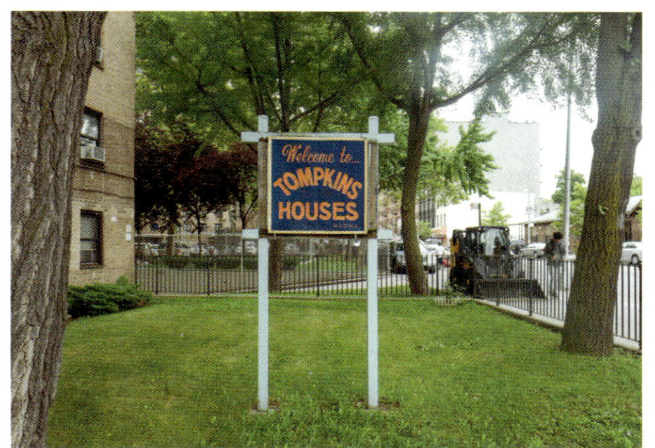
Welcome to...
TOMPKINS
HOUSES
NYCHA

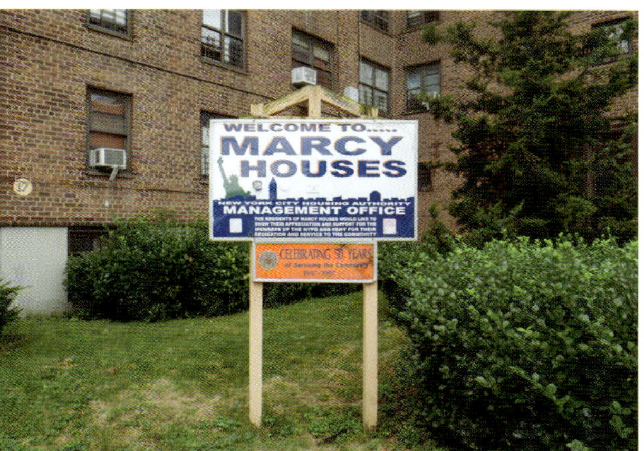
WELCOME TO......
MARCY
HOUSES
NEW YORK CITY HOUSING AUTHORITY
MANAGEMENT OFFICE
CELEBRATING 50 YEARS
of Serving the Community

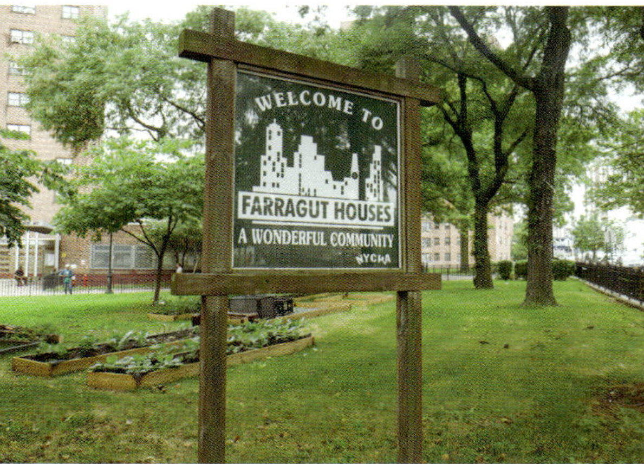
WELCOME TO
FARRAGUT HOUSES
A WONDERFUL COMMUNITY
NYCHA

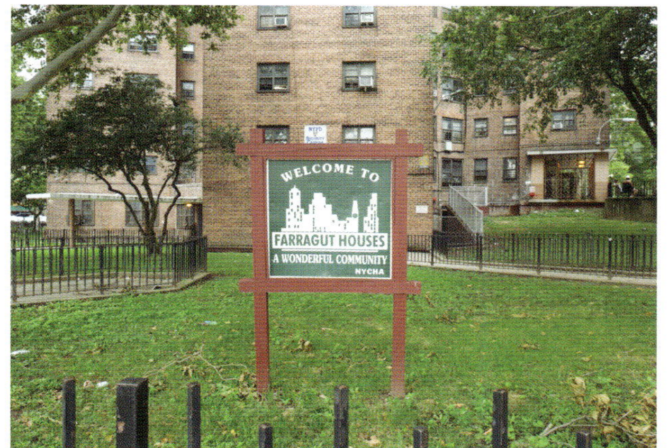

WELCOME TO
FARRAGUT HOUSES
A WONDERFUL COMMUNITY
NYCHA

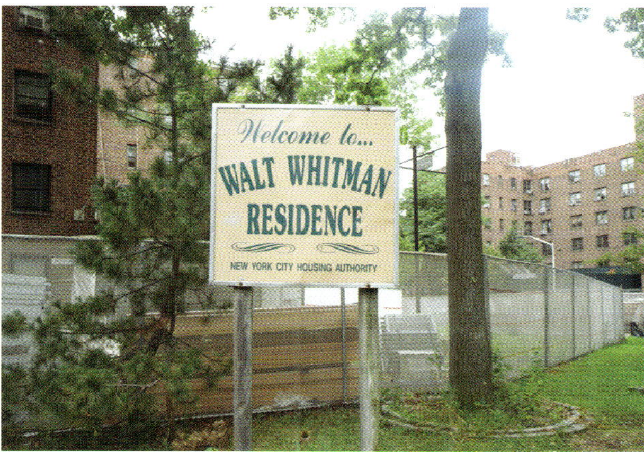

Welcome to...
WALT WHITMAN
RESIDENCE
NEW YORK CITY HOUSING AUTHORITY

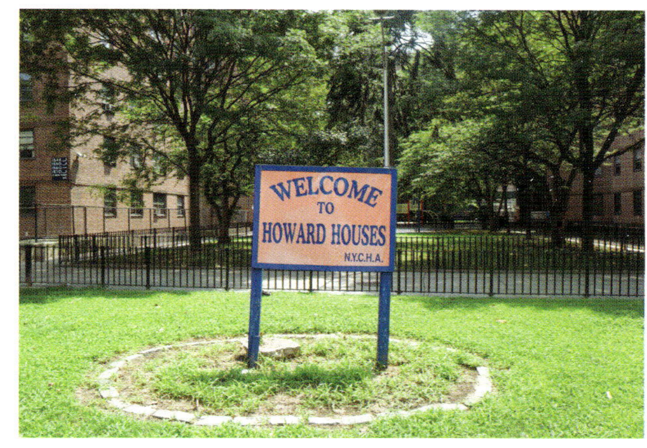

WELCOME
TO
HOWARD HOUSES
N.Y.C.H.A.

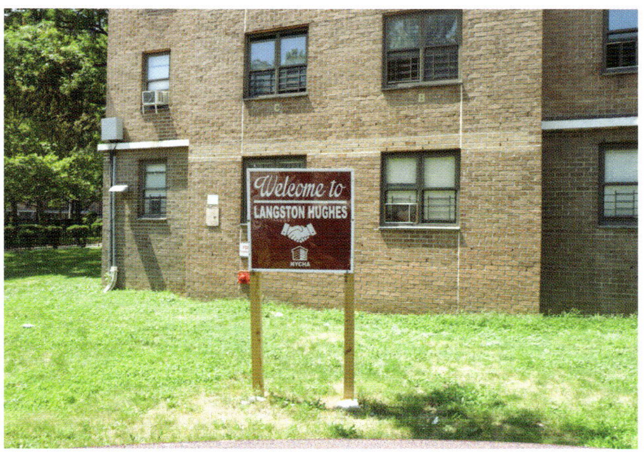

Welcome to...
LANGSTON HUGHES
NYCHA

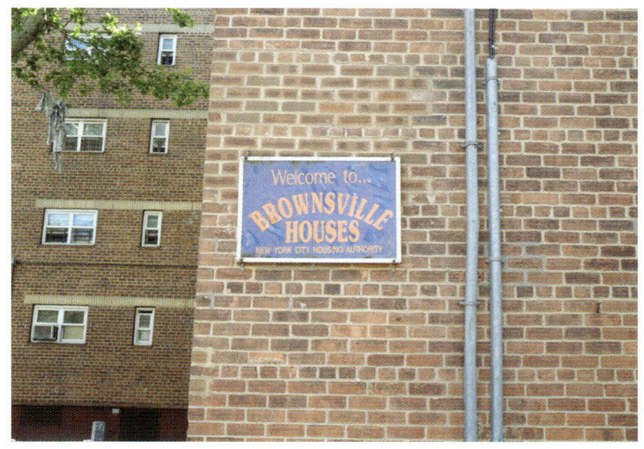

Welcome to...
BROWNSVILLE
HOUSES
NEW YORK CITY HOUSING AUTHORITY

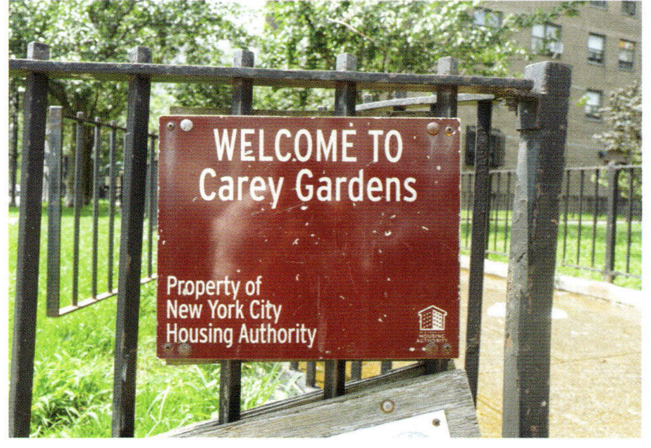

WELCOME TO
Carey Gardens
Property of
New York City
Housing Authority

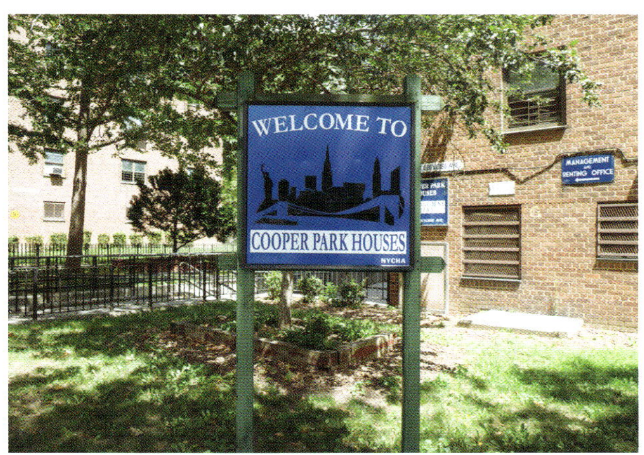

WELCOME TO
COOPER PARK HOUSES
NYCHA
MANAGEMENT
RENTING OFFICE

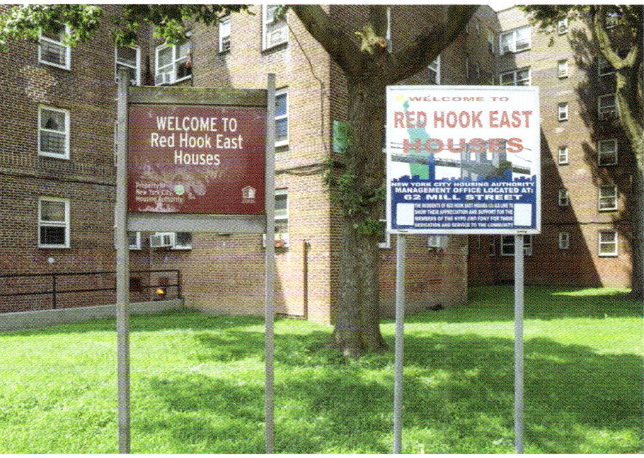

WELCOME TO
Red Hook East
Houses
Property of
New York City
WELCOME TO
RED HOOK EAST
HOUSES
NEW YORK CITY HOUSING AUTHORITY
MANAGEMENT OFFICE LOCATED AT:
62 MILL STREET

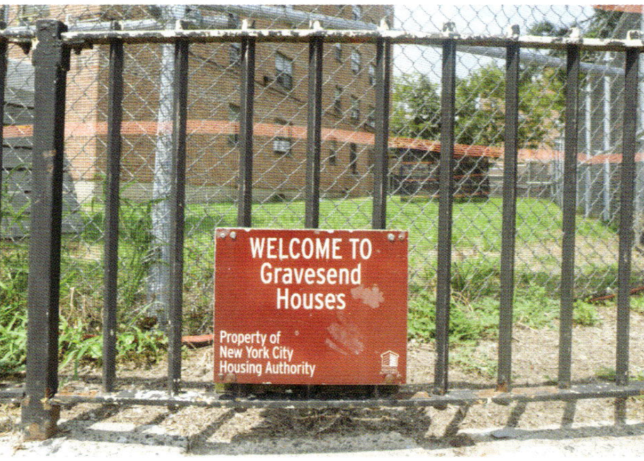

WELCOME TO
Gravesend
Houses
Property of
New York City
Housing Authority

TABLE of CONTENTS

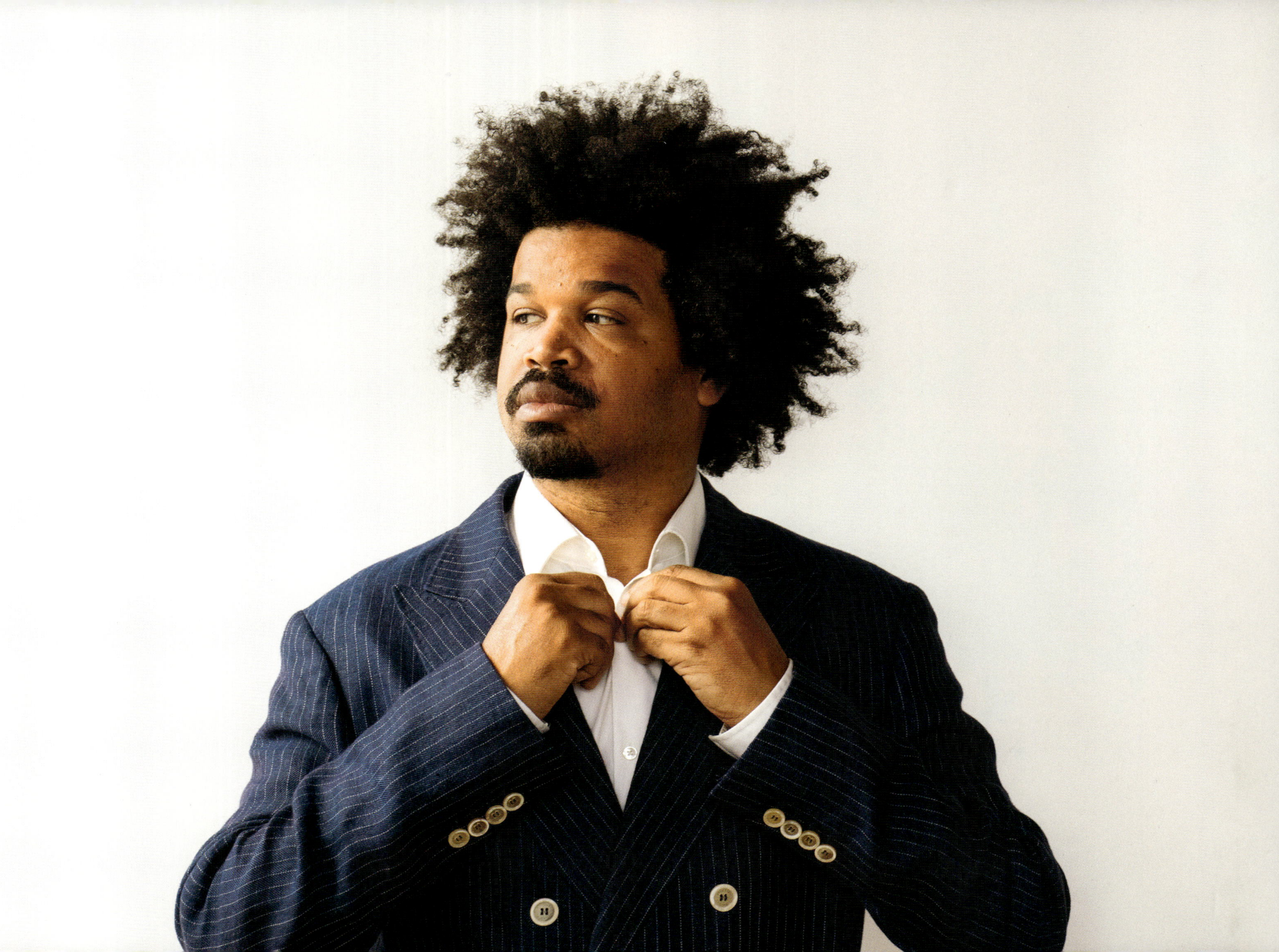

ABOUT THIS BOOK

Documentarian Ian Reid was born and raised in Brooklyn. He grew up in Fort Greene. In 2018 he decided to photograph 23 public housing developments in Brooklyn from above.

His goal was to preserve the architecture and present them as the structures they are without the preconceived notions of what goes on in them. The images are framed by the streets they are defined by and often showing how they look with the changing seasons. This project came to be known as *COMPLEX GEOMETRY* because of one of the many names for public housing. Complex for "Housing Complex" and Geometry for the lines and shapes that became more apparent when viewed from above.

Gentrification and development have changed the surroundings of the public housing - But the buildings and its residents for the most part stay the same.

COMPLEX GEOMETRY respects the true residents of Brooklyn and pays homage to where Reid grew up and still spends a great deal of his time.

COMPLEX GEOMETRY

by Trymaine Lee

Vast stretches of brown-bricked buildings shrug into the Brooklyn sky. They march along for acres in perfect symmetry, parading in lock step to the complex geometry of their own form. Some cut curious, exquisite right angles. Others jaunt in semi-zigs or zags or octagons or cockeyed hashtags, stacked and staggered like dominoes. The low-slung among them jut up from the concrete jungle like jagged garden bricks. While the high-rises threaten the clouds.

These hulking titans aren't the quintessential three and four-story brownstone houses for which Brooklyn is famed. No, these are "the Projects," as they've come to be known, a series of public housing developments that were erected across the city nearly a century ago. They gave solace to low-income and working-class families, many of them immigrants, who churned the cogs of this tireless, mechanical city. But the projects have always been more than just places to live. They're an idea as much as they are a destination. These massive, often clunkily designed buildings not only altered the topography of New York City, but the city's imagination. And it's very soul. They've been places of redemption and rejection, an amorphous of everything beautiful and ugly and unforgiving about this city.

The story of public housing in New York, and what these buildings have come to represent, is the story of perpetual two-ness: rich and poor, black and white, humanity and inhumanity, the logical and irrational, their ubiquity and to some degree, their invisibility, blending into the background of a city with little attention or living space to spare. With names like Breukelen, Farragut, Ingersoll and Wyckoff Gardens, these complexes offer an air of aristocracy. But their history is humbling.

In 1936, New York City Mayor Fiorello La Guardia hailed the razing of huge swaths of slumland and crumbling tenement buildings to make room for a sprawling new series of public housing developments, among the first of their kind in the United States.

"Tear down the old, build up the new," he said. "Down with rotten antiquated rat holes. Down with hovels, down with disease, down with fire traps, let in the sun, let in the sky, a new day is dawning, a new life, a new America."

The U.S. was in the middle of the Great Depression and people in many of the city's toughest neighborhoods were languishing in squalid, over-populated tenement buildings. The New York City Housing Authority was established to design, construct and serve as administrator of the new complexes. The projects were meant to be a temporary respite to help hard luck and hard working families get back on their feet. Just a year before La Guardia's grand proclamation of sun light and sunny skies, the first of these developments sprouted up on the Lower East Side of Manhattan. It was christened the First Houses and those first 122 apartments — with rents adjusted to each family's monthly income — would indeed usher in a new day for New York City.

The projects, as actual edifices and ideas are at once a flex of New Deal-era architectural ingenuity and in more recent years a shorthand for poverty, crime and violence. They were designed New York City-Big, but their footprint has always been felt locally. They shaped the social and communal life of residents and everyone in their orbit, neighborhood-by-neighborhood. These developments, many housing thousands, were meant as a springboard for struggling families to get ahead, but over the decades residents would become much poorer and more intransient. City and federal funding and maintenance of the developments would become inconsistent at best and lacking at worst. Their foundation, much like America's, had been built on racism and segregation. Early on there were projects intended for whites and those for Blacks, though class lines sometimes blurred the much deeper and more intrinsic racial divide. White flight would deepen segregation not simply within public housing but of public housing. Until the late 1950s the majority of residents were ethnic whites -- Irish, Italians and Jews mostly. The building of additional developments, and in turn, aggressive neighborhood clearance that included many disinvested in Black and brown communities, dislodged countless people already struggling to find affordable housing. The projects became home for large numbers of them.

 Today, more than 560,000 New York City residents, 1 in 15, live in public housing, though the actual number could be much higher. In fact, if public housing tenants were to form their own city, it would have a larger population than Atlanta, Kansas City, Miami, New Orleans and Oakland. NYCHA operates 316 separate developments, including 173,762 apartments in 2,351 residential buildings across the 5 boroughs. Brooklyn boasts the highest public housing population in New York. More than 90% of NYCHA residents are Black or Hispanic. And while for decades much of public housing was concentrated in low-income minority neighborhoods, 85% of those same developments are now located in high-income gentrifying communities.

Much of what we understand about life as it's lived in public housing comes from those on the ground, from families who've spent generations bound in their walls, or those who used them to climb to greater heights. Or from the media, whose lens is often jaundiced by hysterical accounts of bad things happening to bad people in bad neighborhoods.

In so many ways that view, our view, is myopic. It's limited in as much as our own humanity— filtered through what we can see, touch, taste and smell— organizes our understanding of the world in which we live. In that sense we are mere mortals, arrogant, small and ant-like. And New York City is filled with ants who easily take the size and scope of everything in this turbulent, mega-city for granted.

From street level, the fundamental nature of the projects is easily lost in what we think we see in them. The history. The contradictions. The allusions.

But what if we could see them from an alternate vantage point? What if we were able to see beyond our limits, literally?

Photographer and documentarian Ian Reid gives us that gift. In this book, Complex Geometry, Reid delivers a god's-eye view of these Brooklyn behemoths. We're wings as his camera lens soars hundreds of feet above some of the largest public housing complexes in New York to examine the unseen intricacy of their design.

The vision for this project began in 2015 as Reid gazed out of a window during a return flight back to the New York City. The shapes of the buildings he saw down below and their repetition, sparked something inside of him. It was the physical construct of the buildings that moved him as an artist, no doubt. But there was also a bigger idea tugging at him, one that questioned the social construct that the projects' buildings represented. They were these islands of poverty and marginalization surrounded by extraordinary wealth and excess.

During his research Reid kept coming back to questions of "who designed these buildings and for who." He read books on people like Robert Moses, the notorious "master builder" who for decades used the unfettered power and influence afforded him via political appointment to literally reshape New York City. He constructed tunnels and zoos and beaches. Lincoln Center and the United Nations. In all he reportedly built 416 miles of highways and 13 bridges among other architectural feats. But nearly everything he touched was tinged with racism. To keep Black beachgoers from visiting the newly built Jones Beach, he designed parkway overpasses too low for buses to pass under, given that most African Americans used public transit at the time. He used highways to keep Black and white neighborhoods cleaved apart. Yet, of all the ways he used design to reinforce segregation, it's the projects that have stood the test of time. While Reid's work focuses on the visual, the shapes, what's seen, the unseen forces that have also shaped the projects and life in them permeate Complex Geometry.

What Reid reveals in this very specific view of the world and the borough of his birth, is a grand and complicated experiment, an equation that in some way binds us all.

"I wanted to share an interesting point of view of my city that hasn't been shown in a concentrated way," says Reid, who was born and raised in Brooklyn's Fort Greene neighborhood. "I'm from Brooklyn. As a kid growing up I heard lots of stories about all of these different places. I don't think people really understand just how complex living there is for people. It might seem very simple but none of this is simple at all."

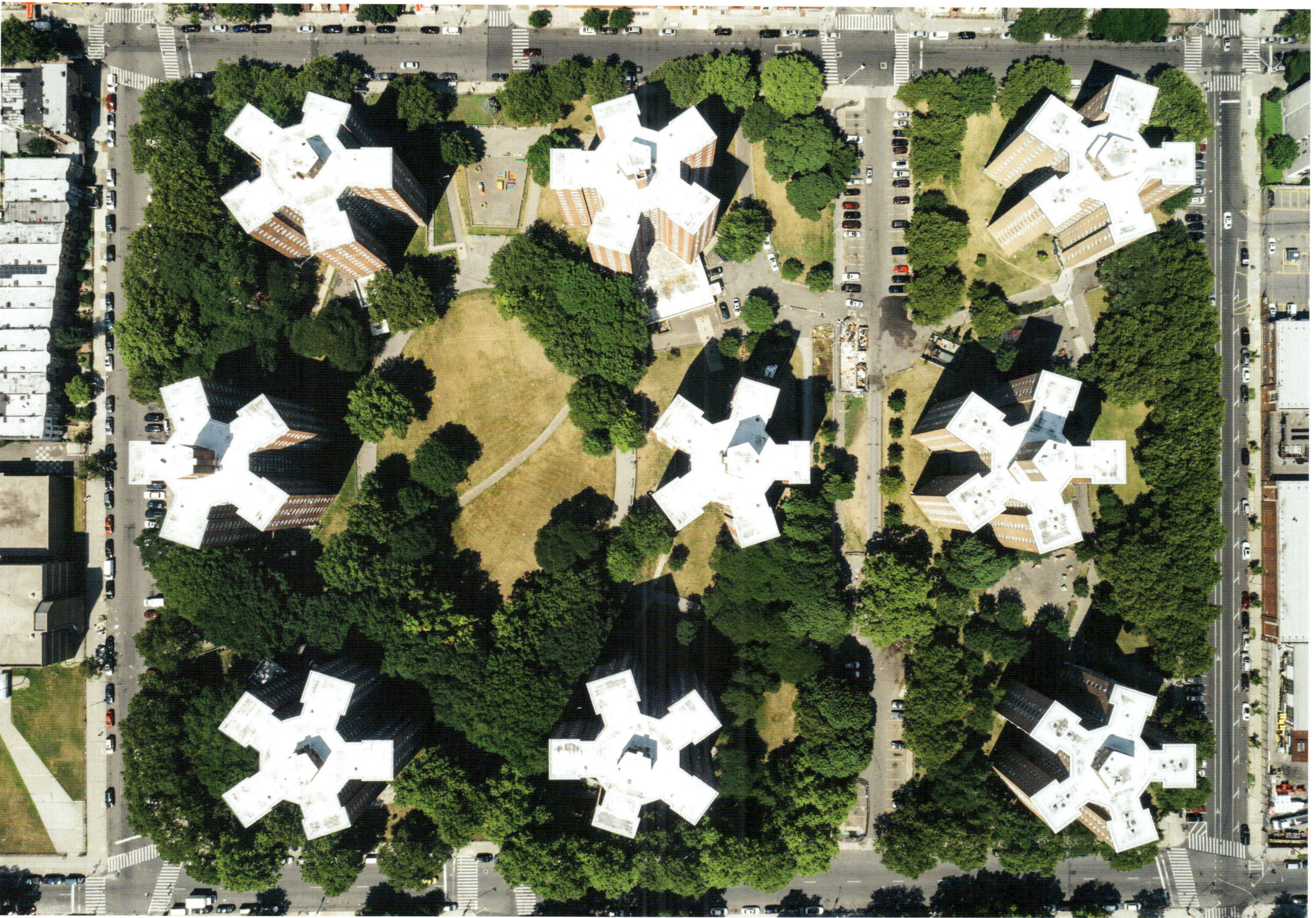

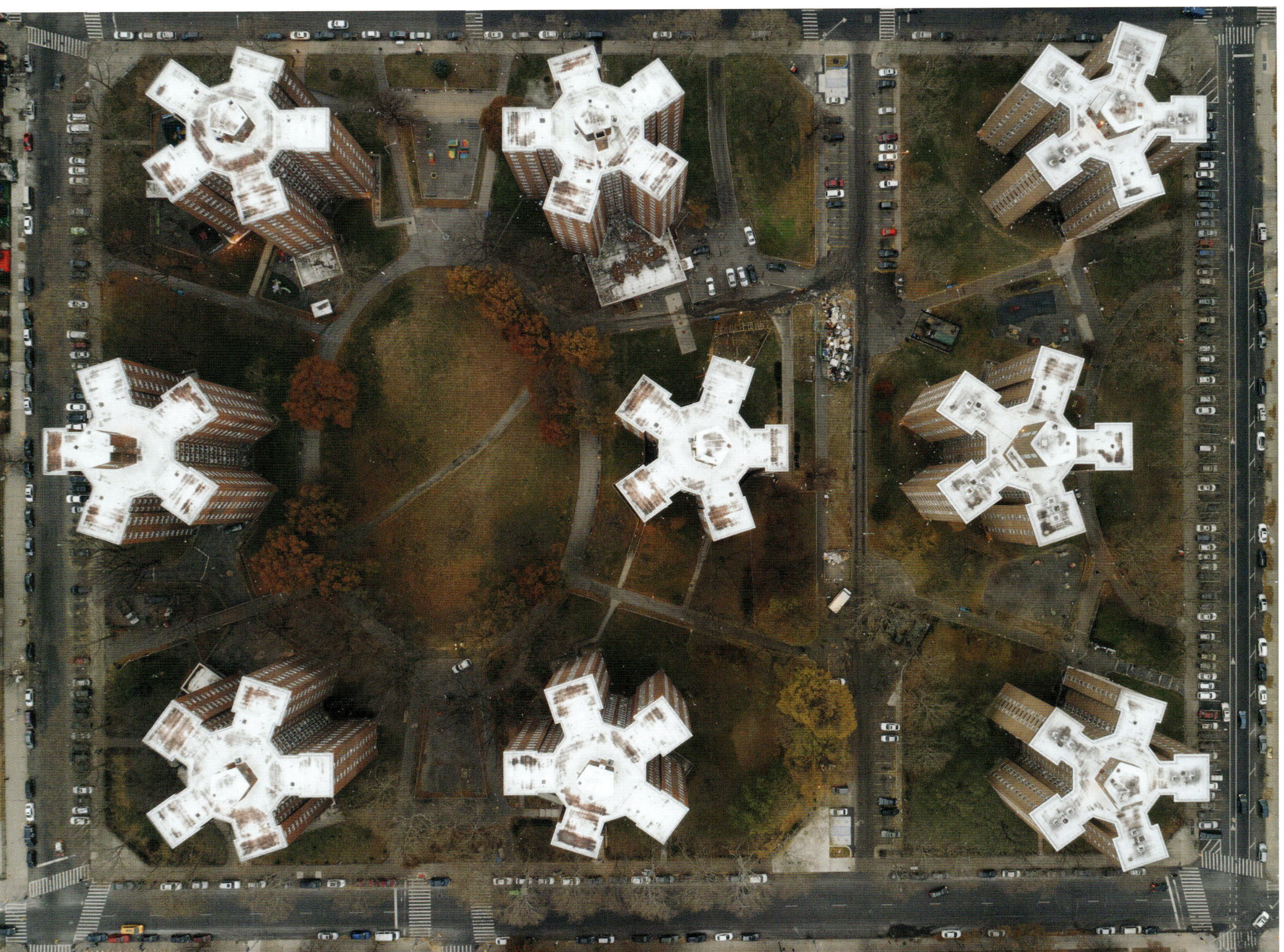

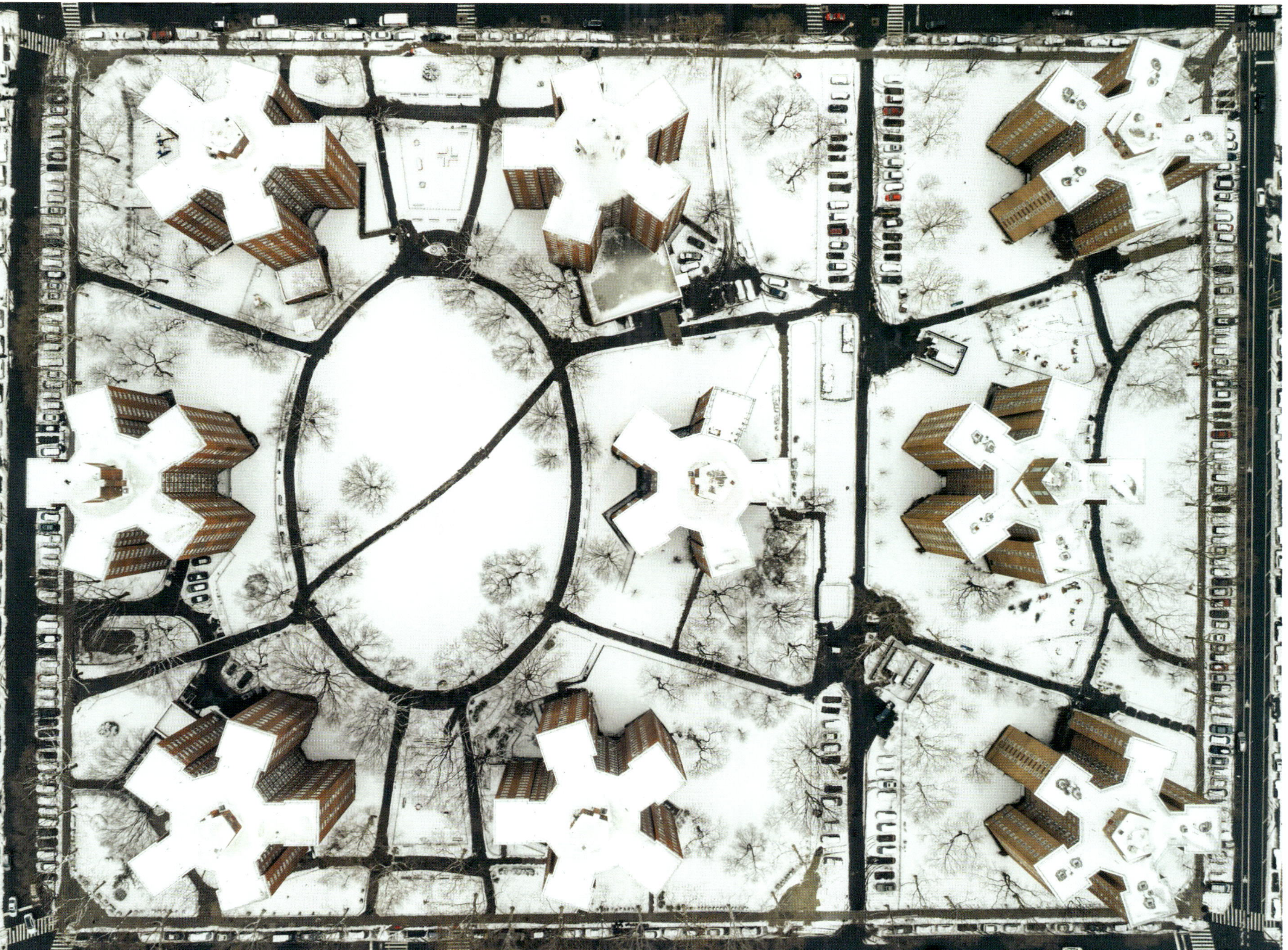

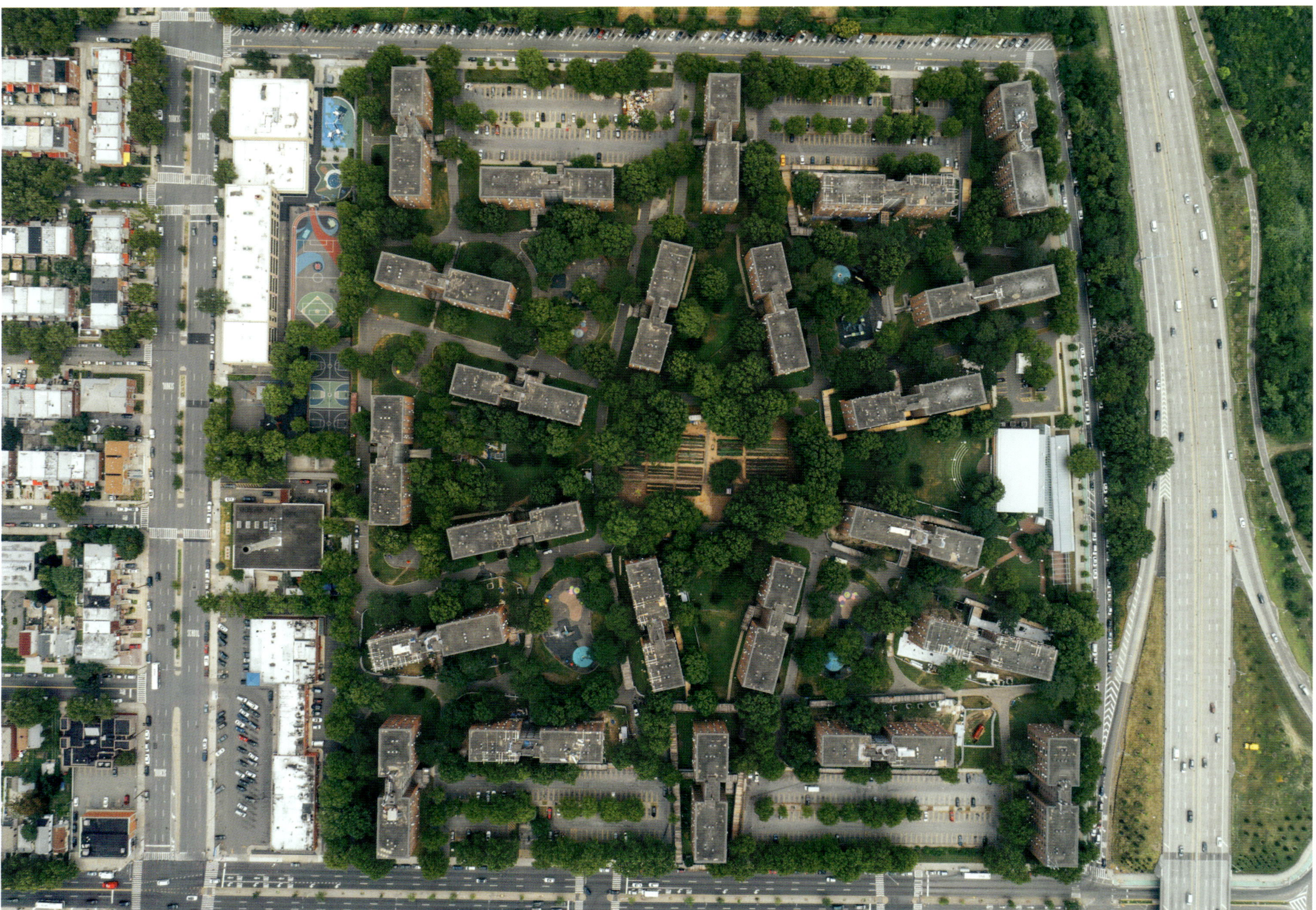

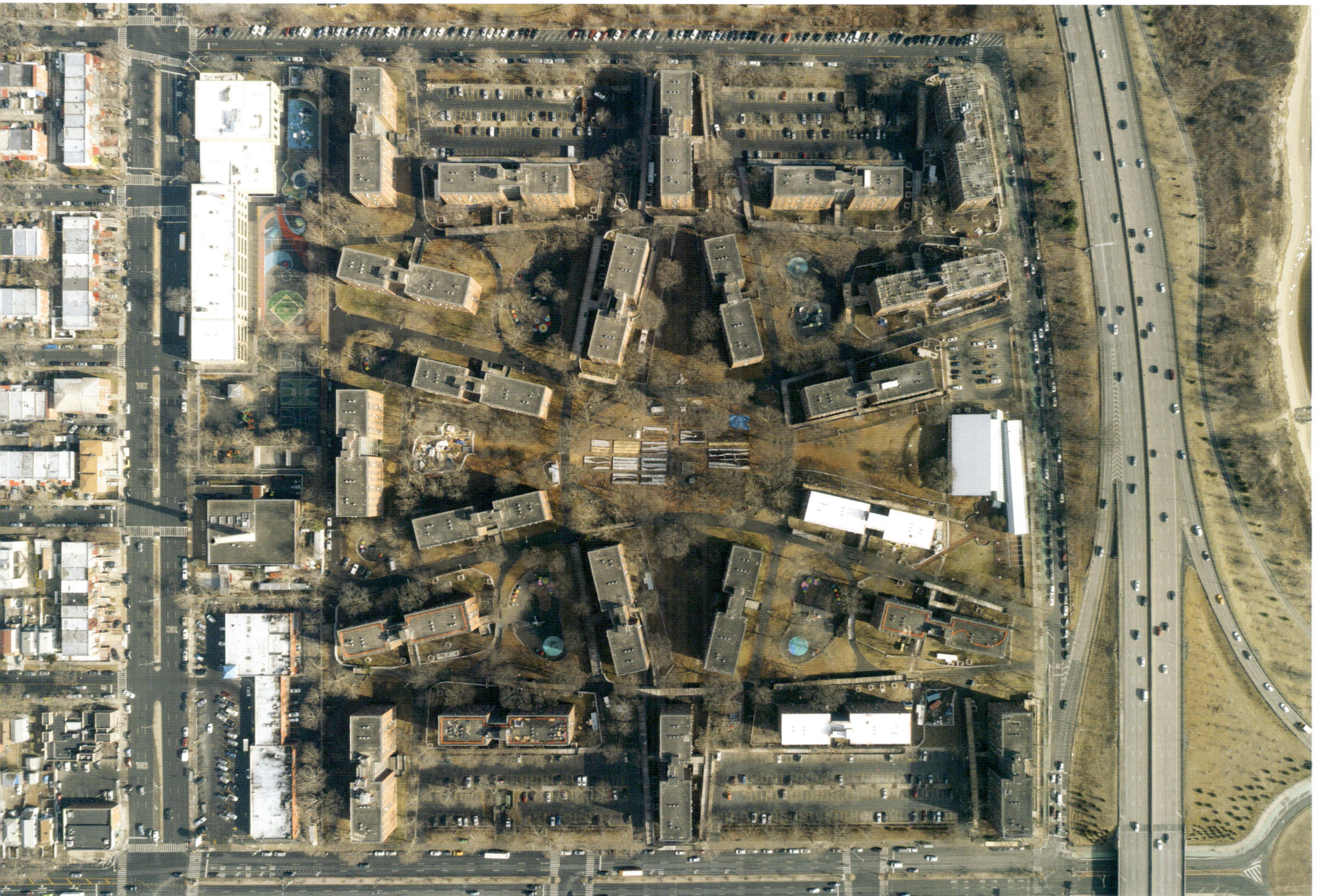

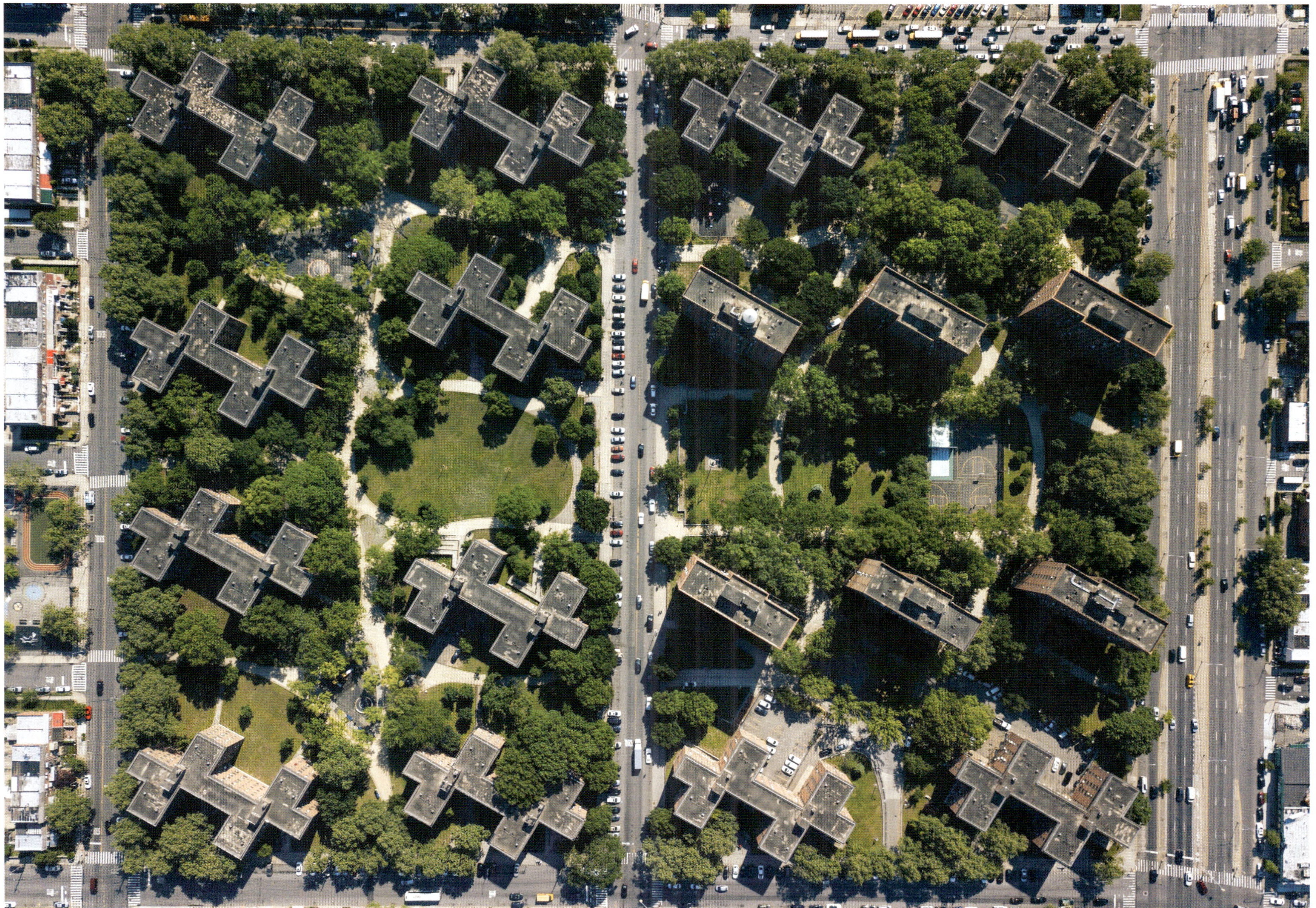

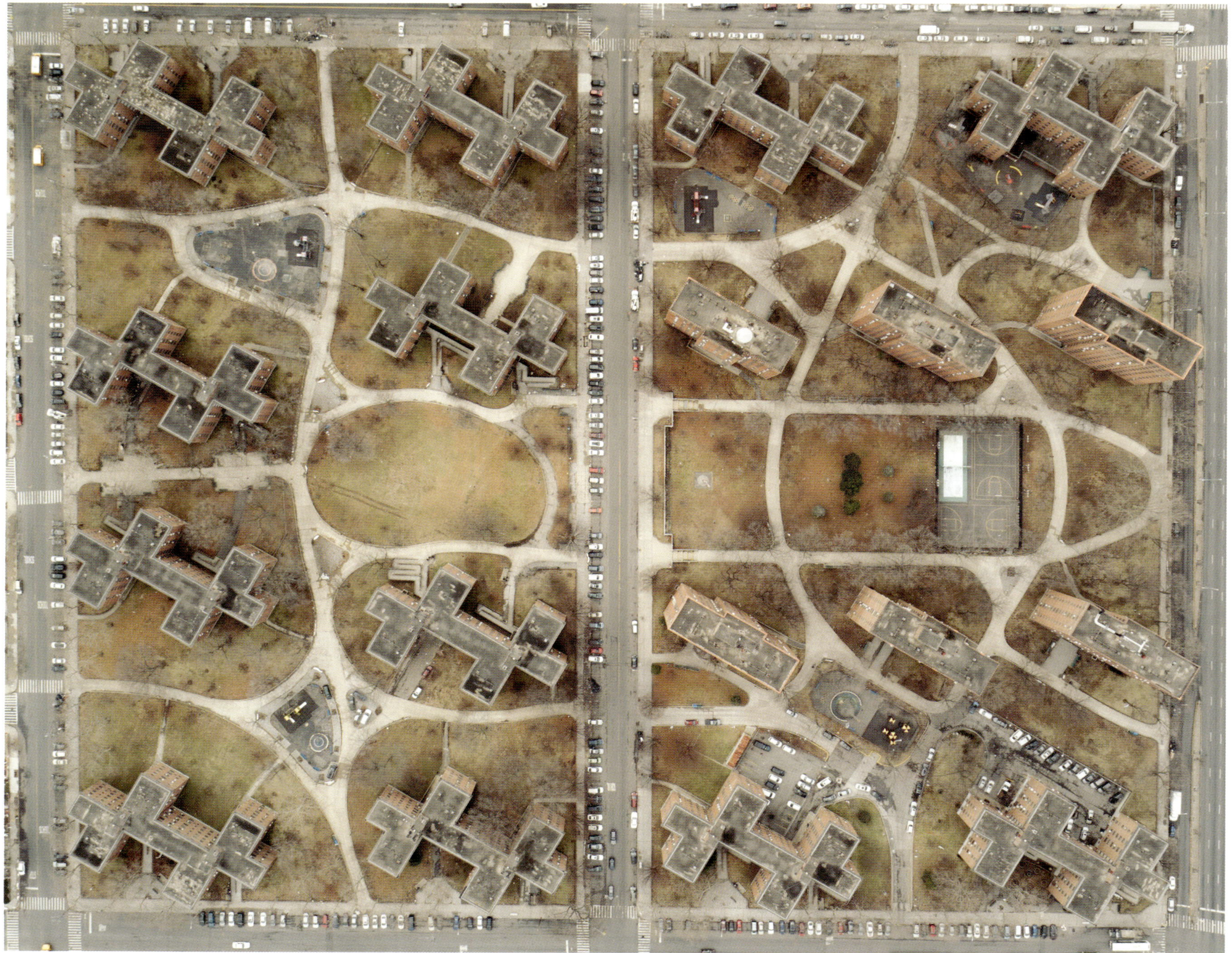

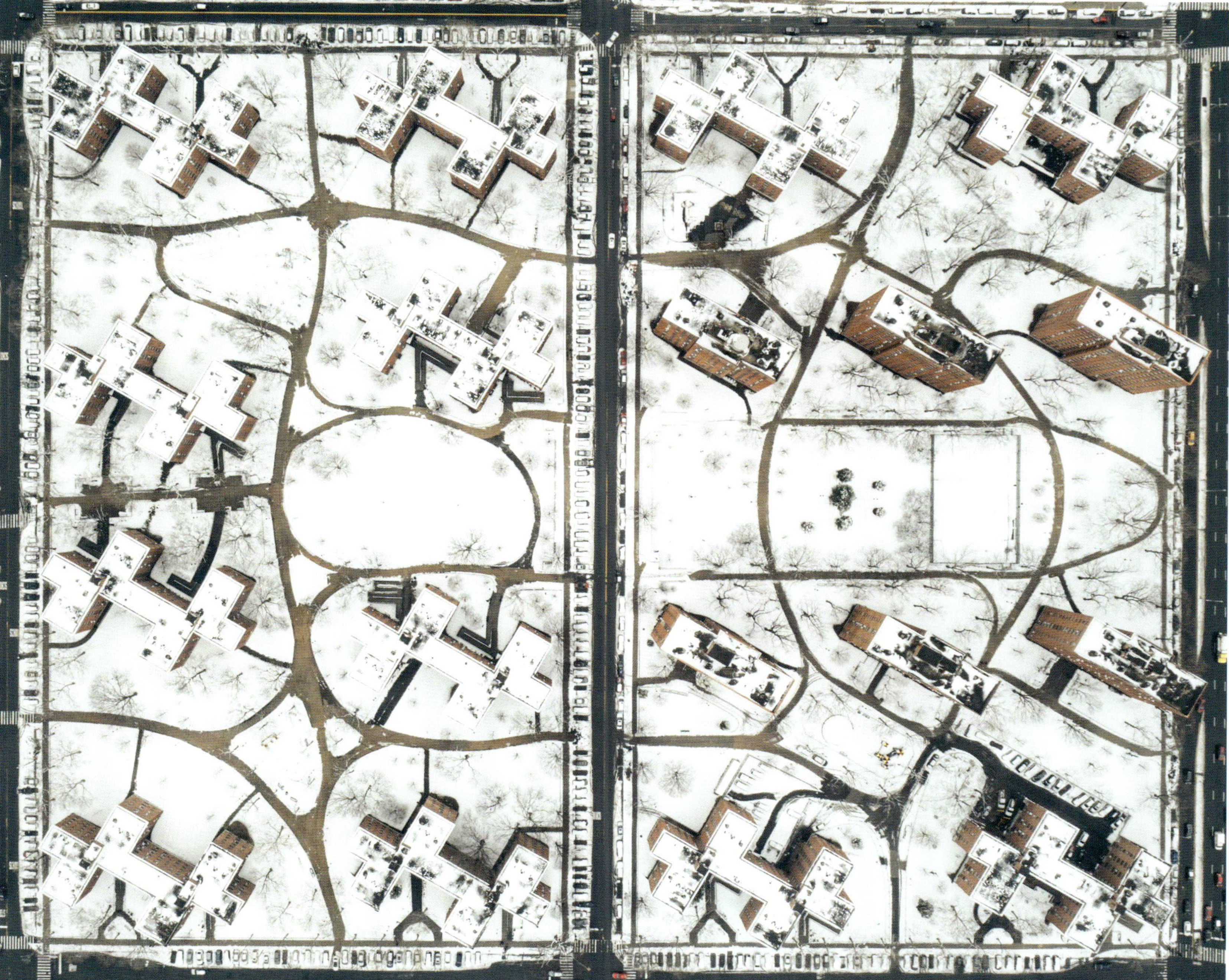

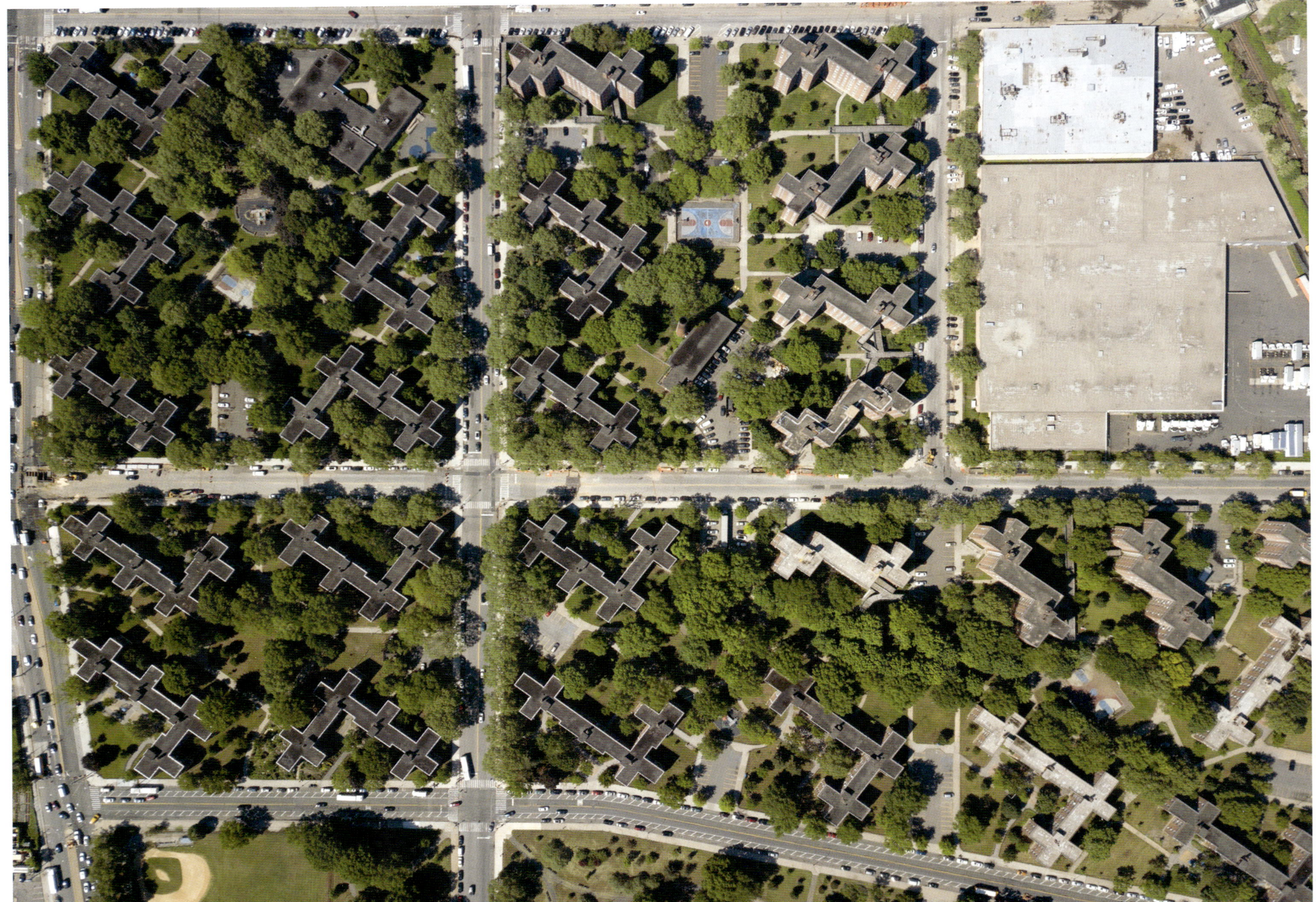

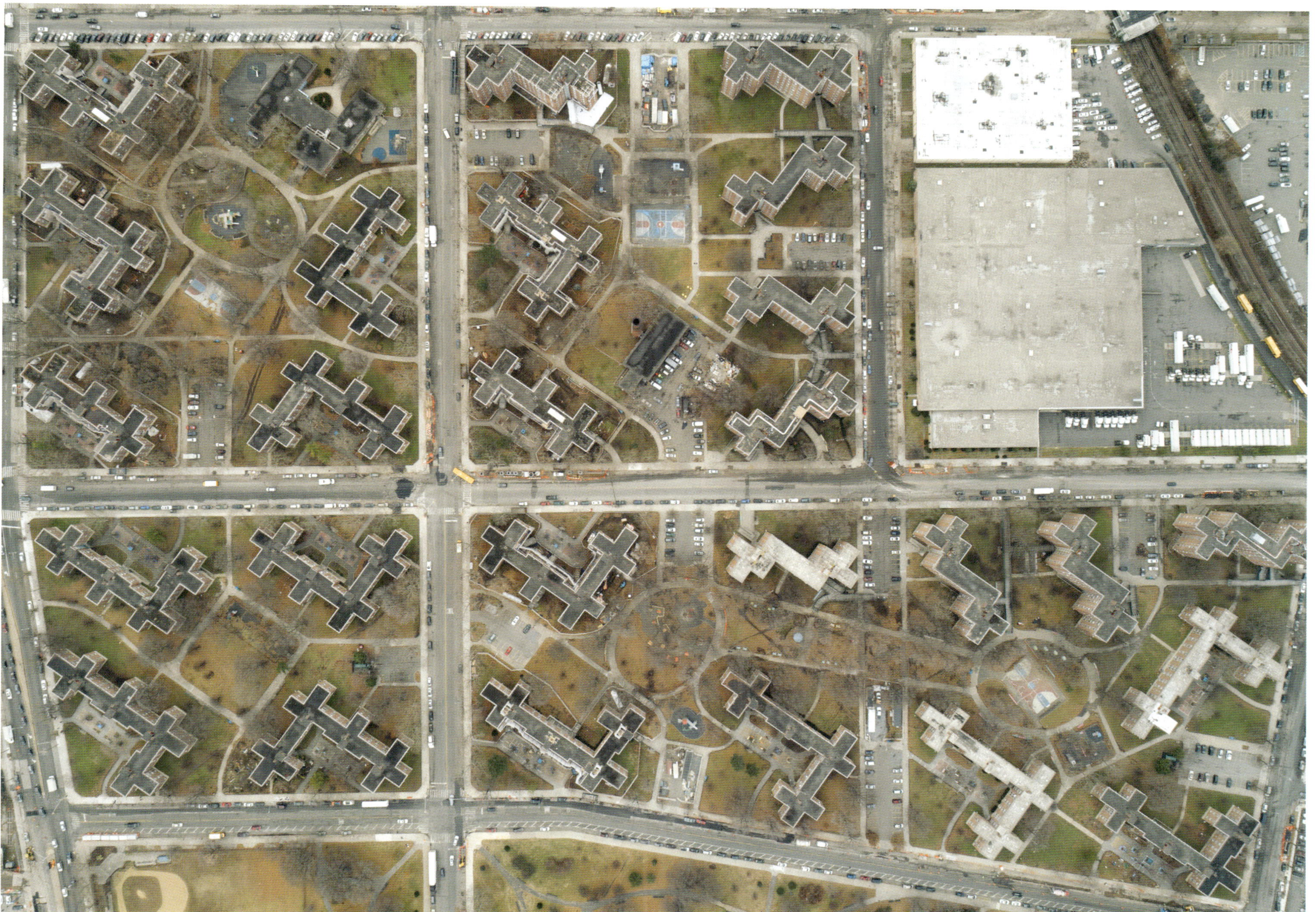

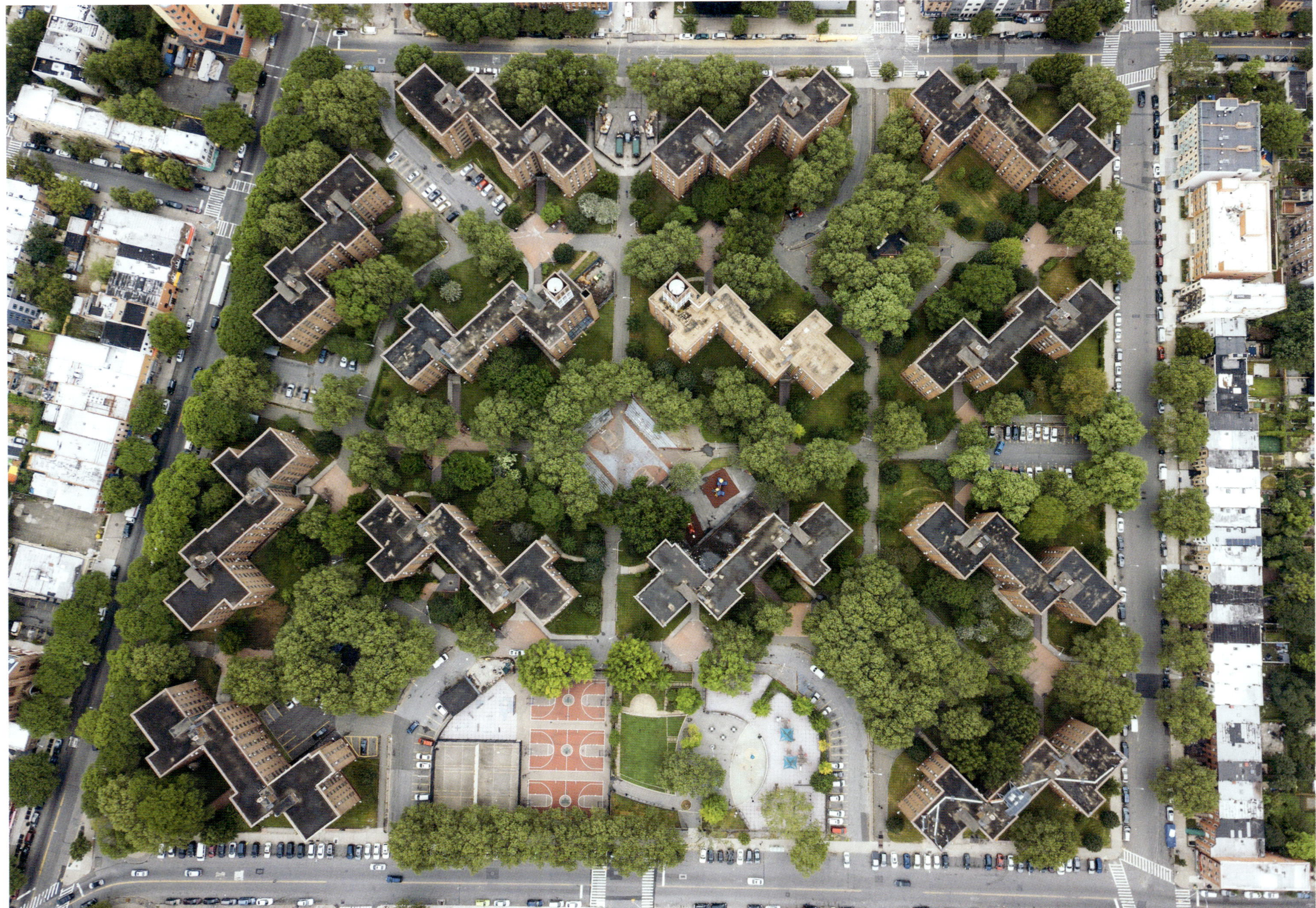

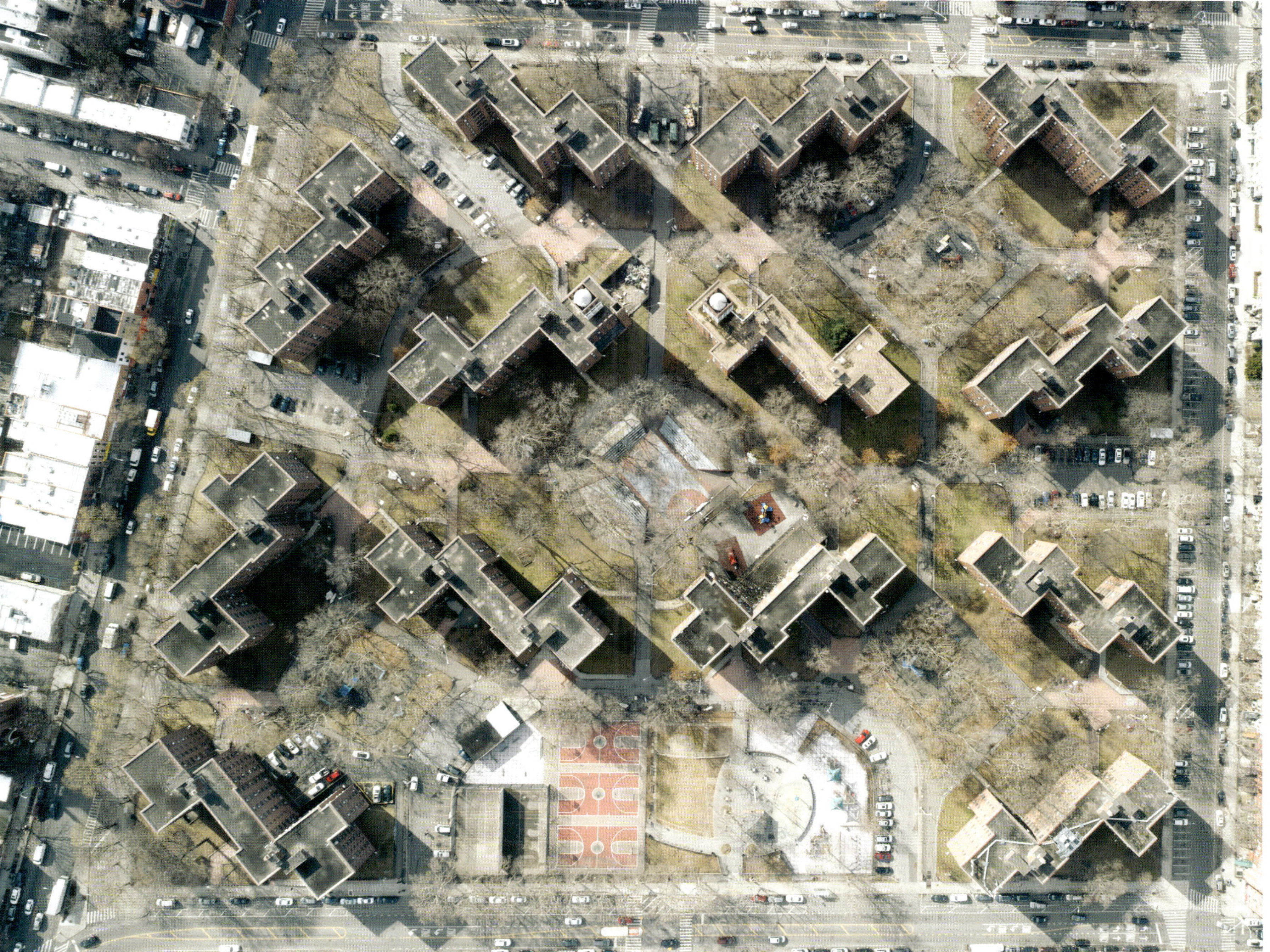

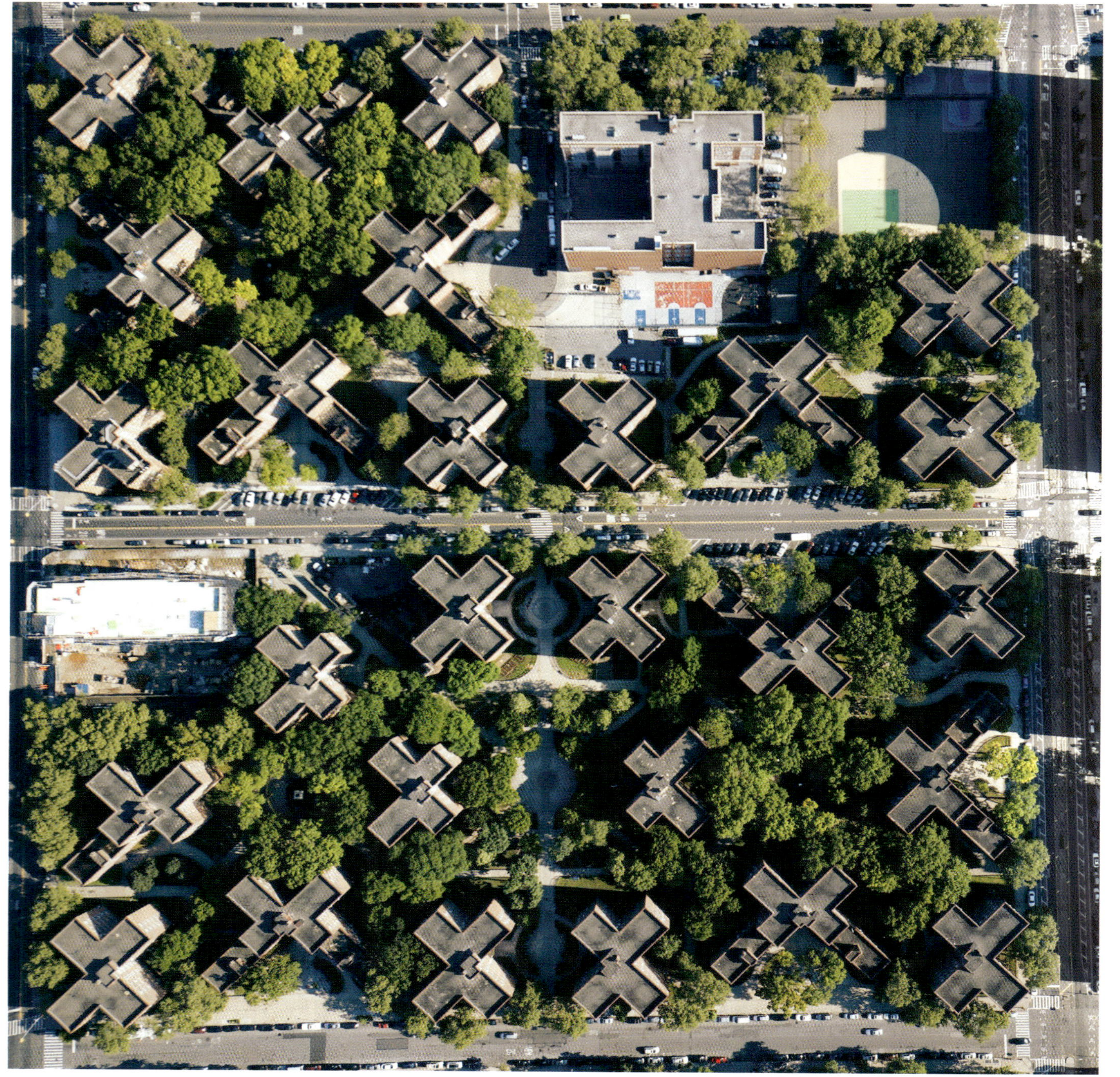

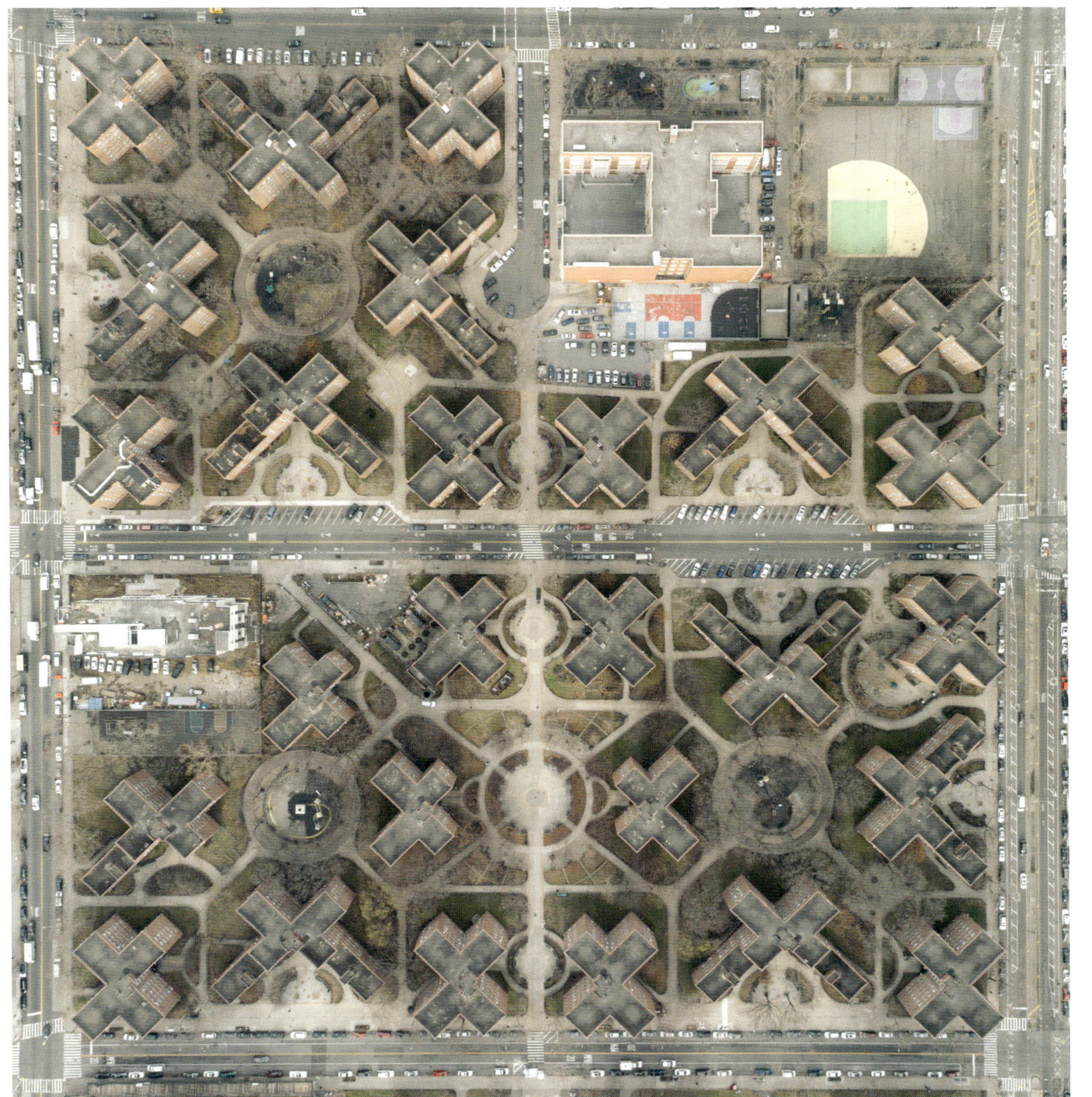

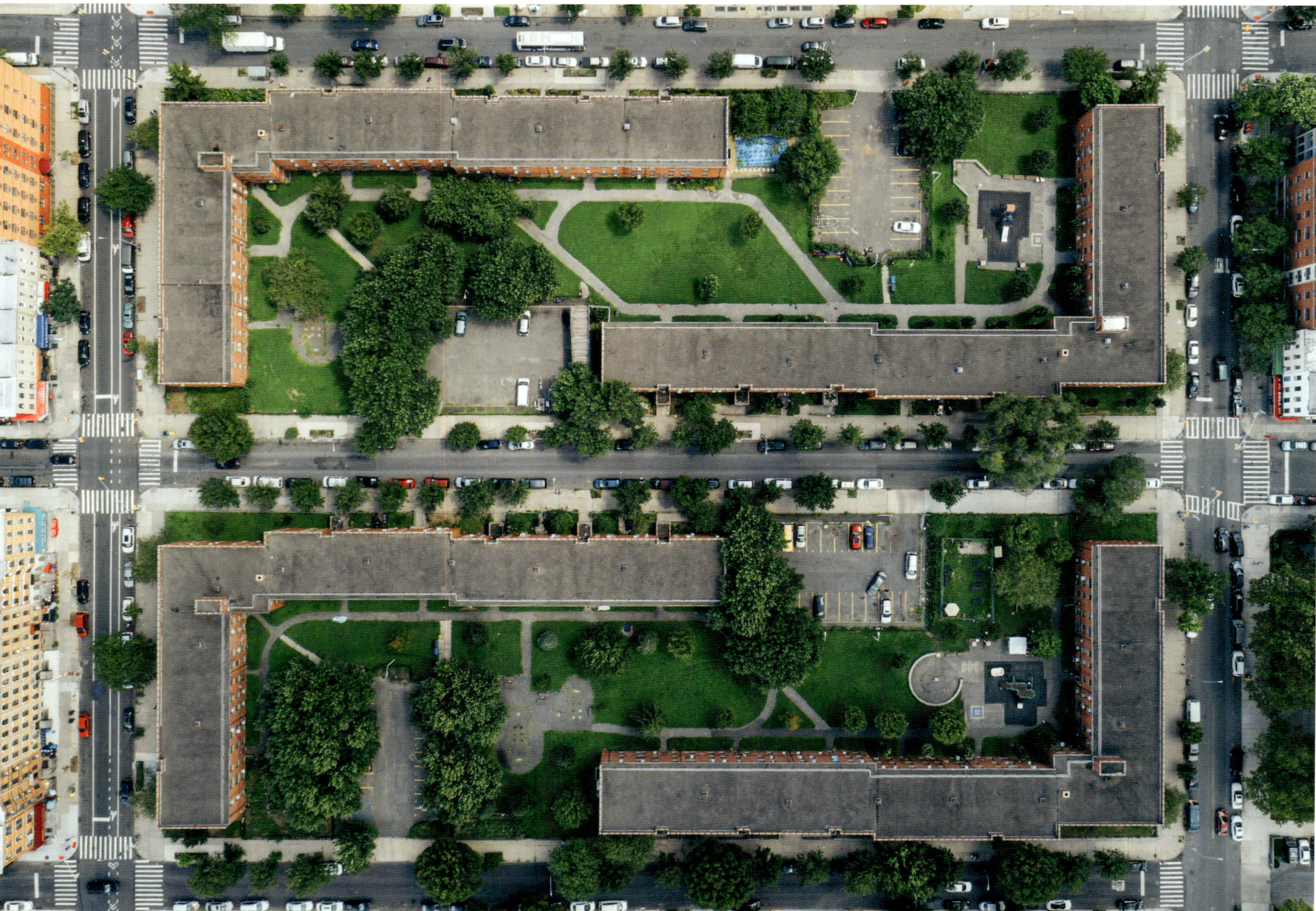

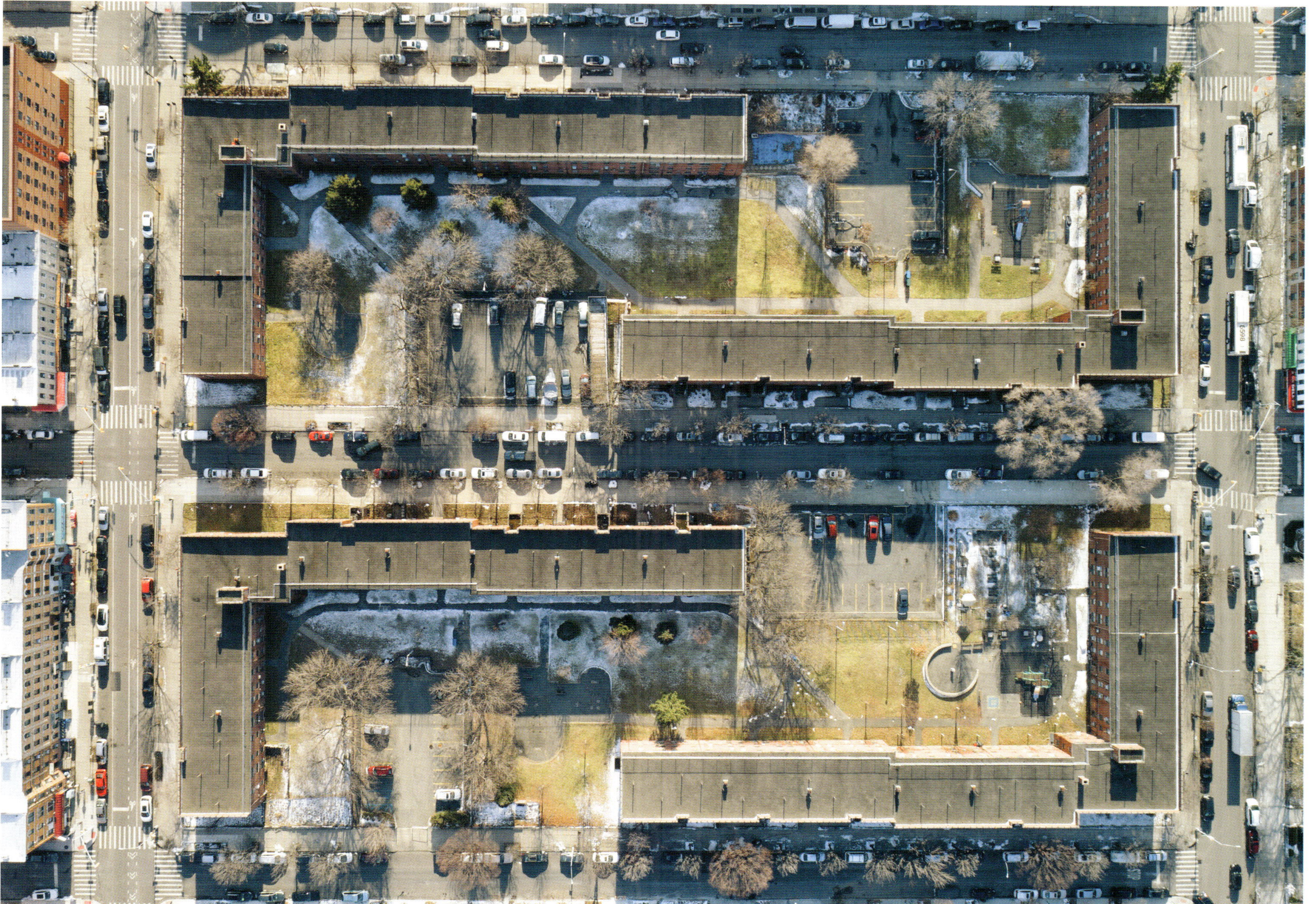

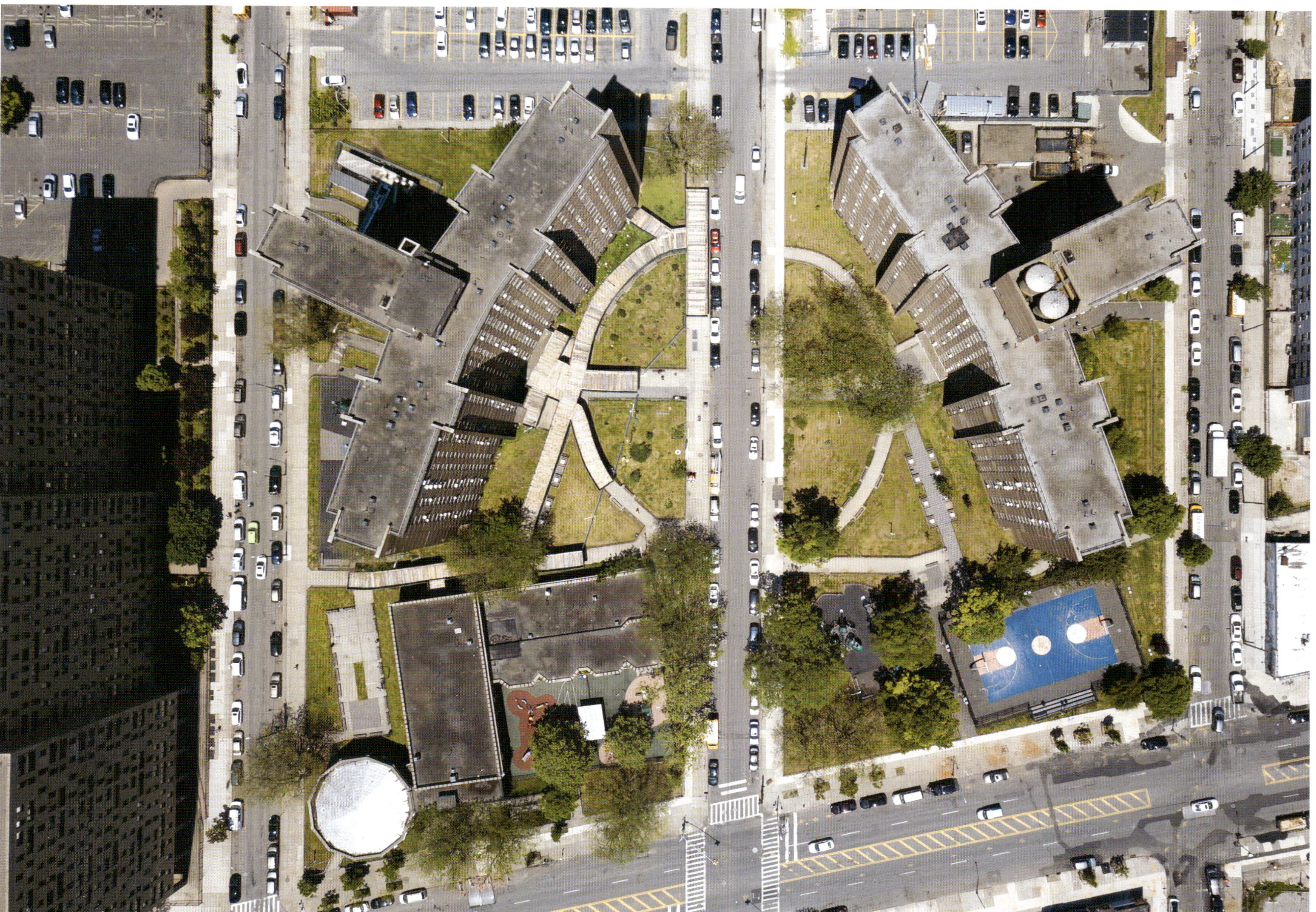

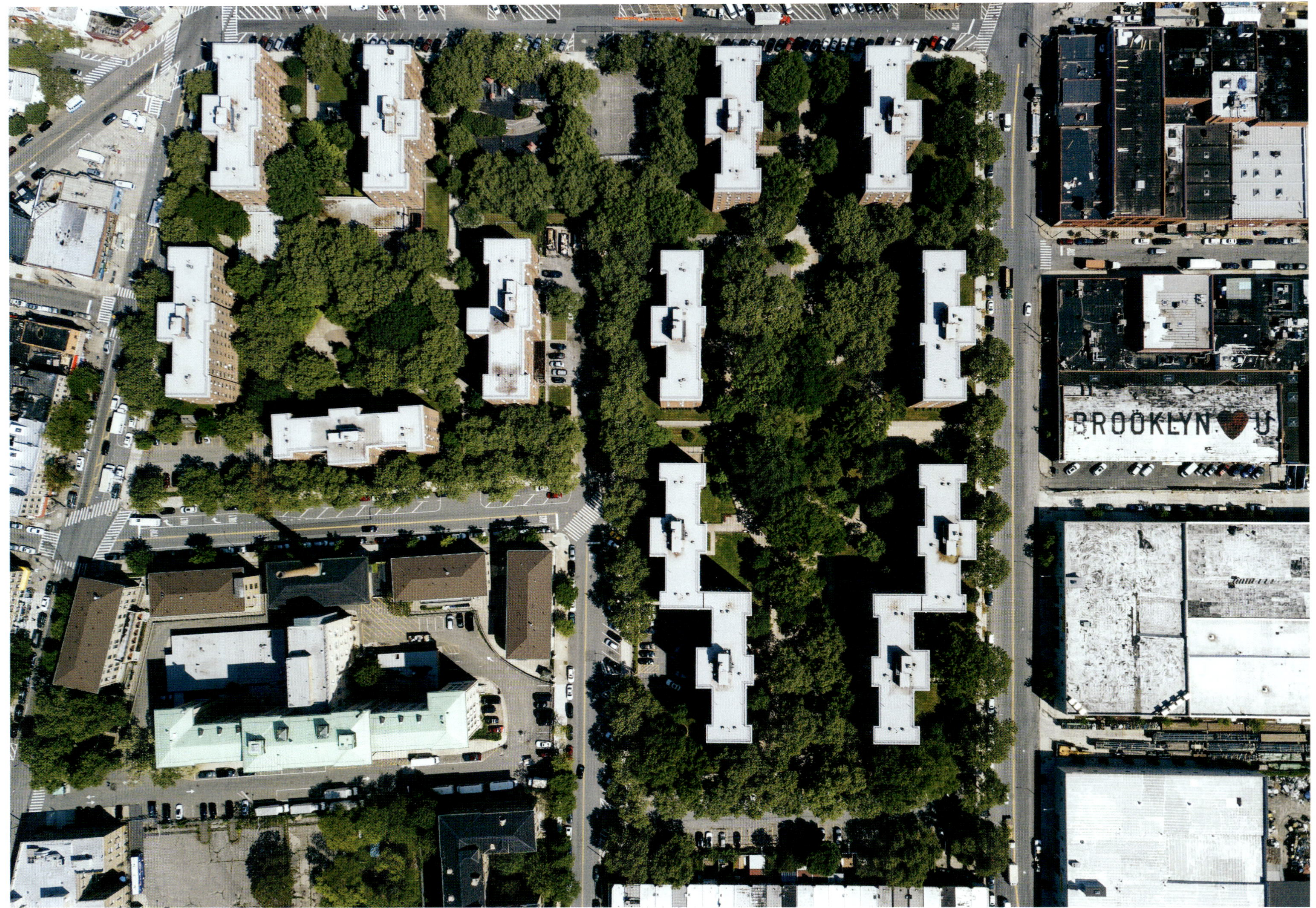
BROOKLYN ♥ U

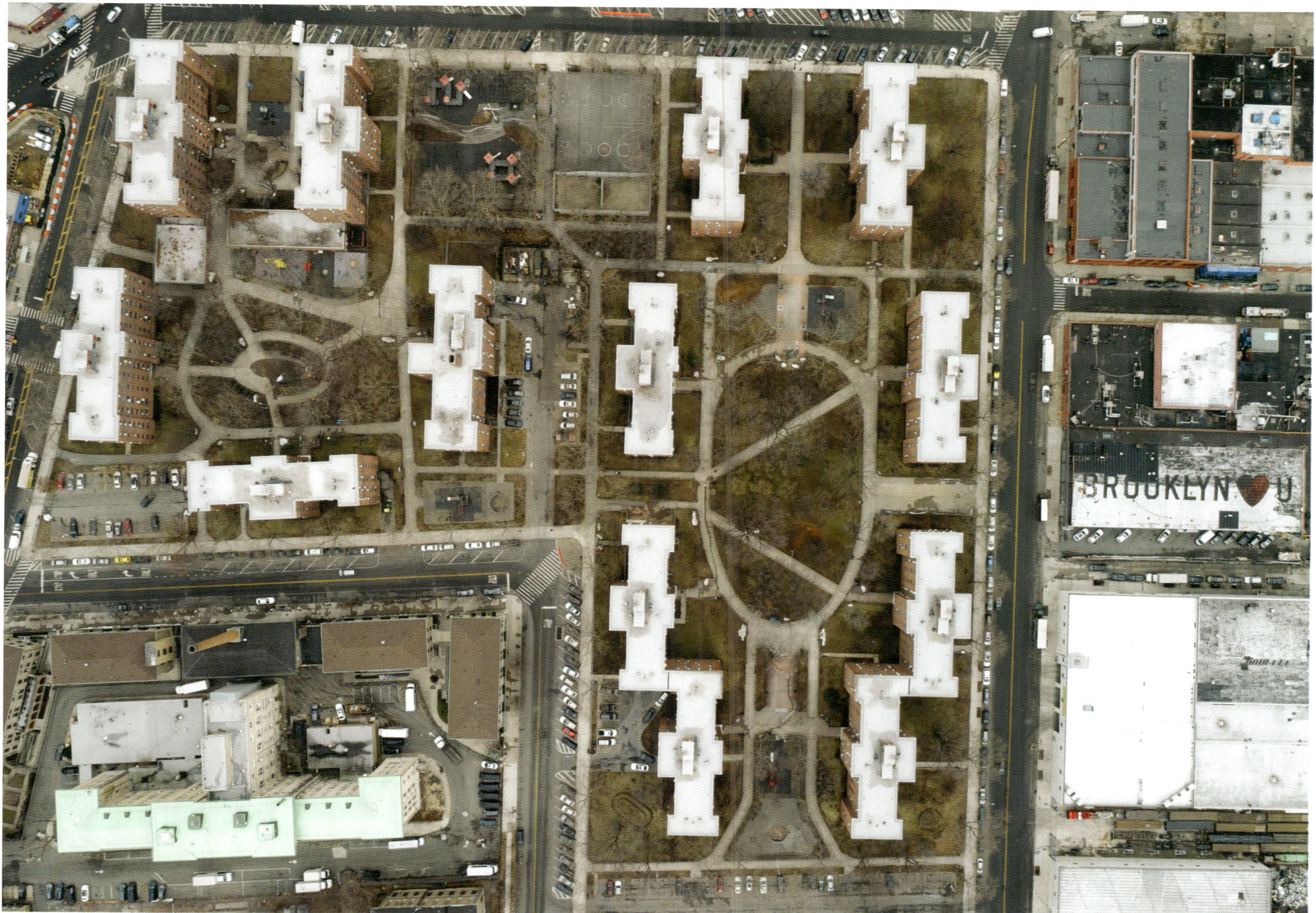
BROOKLYN ♥ U

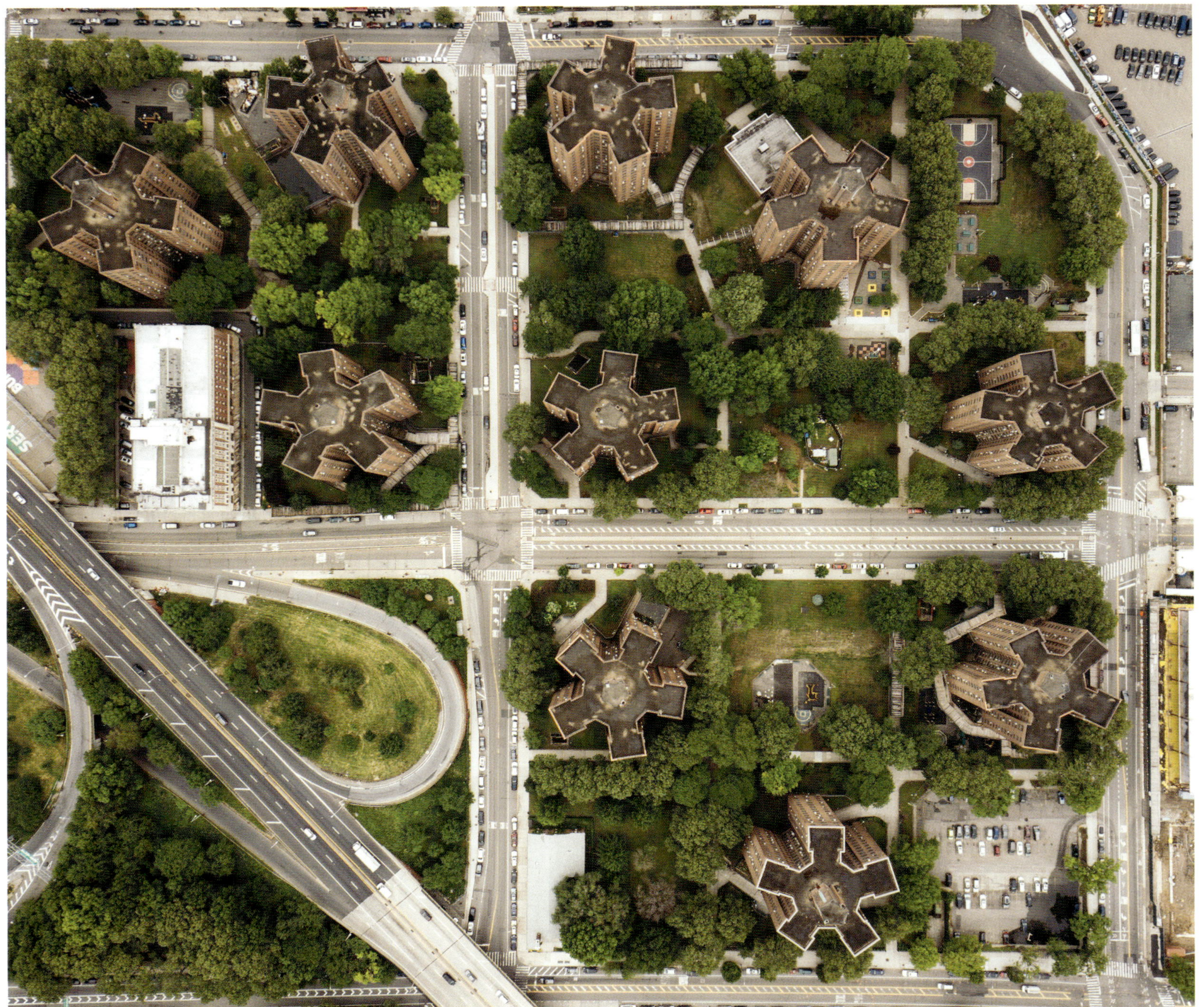

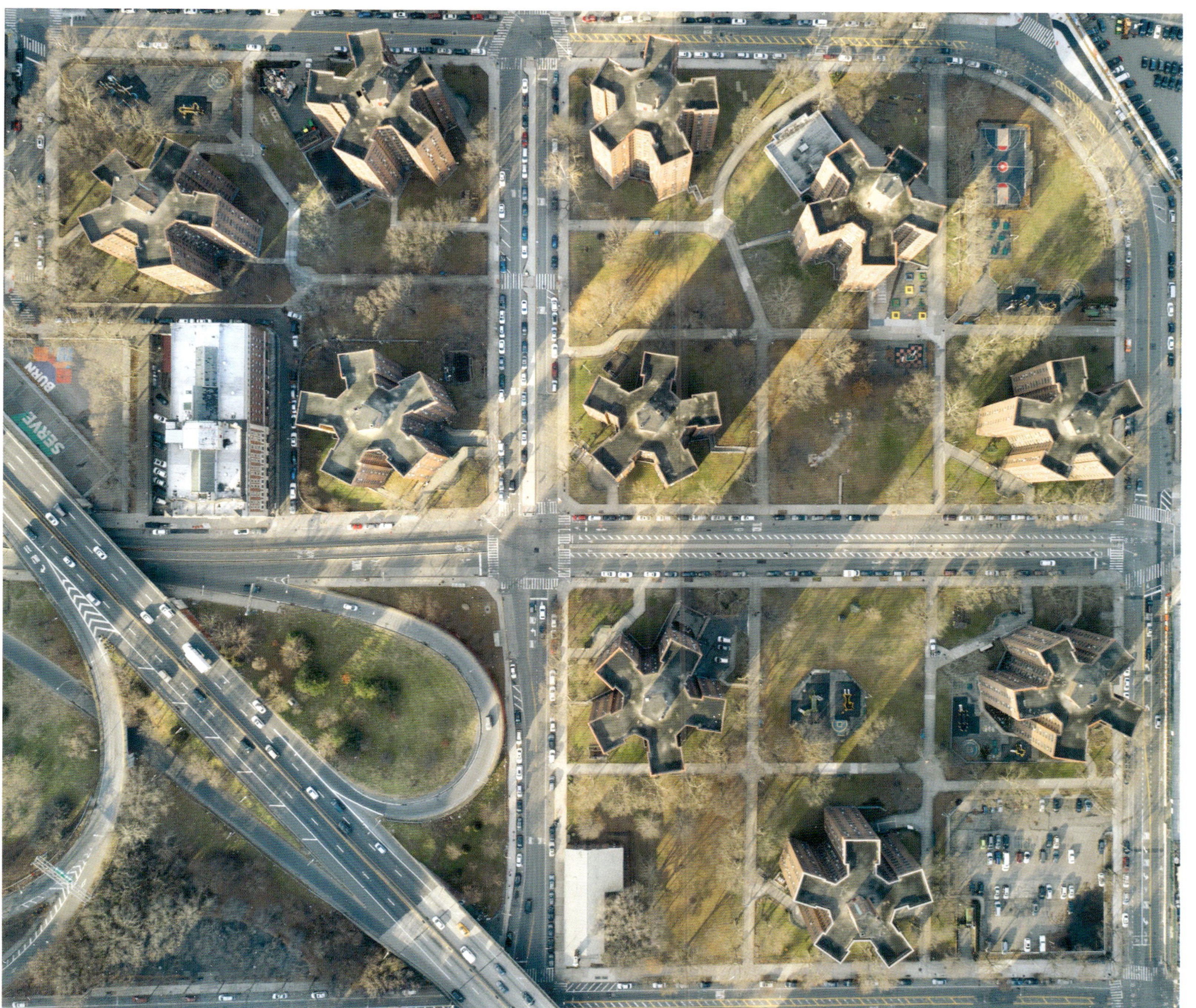

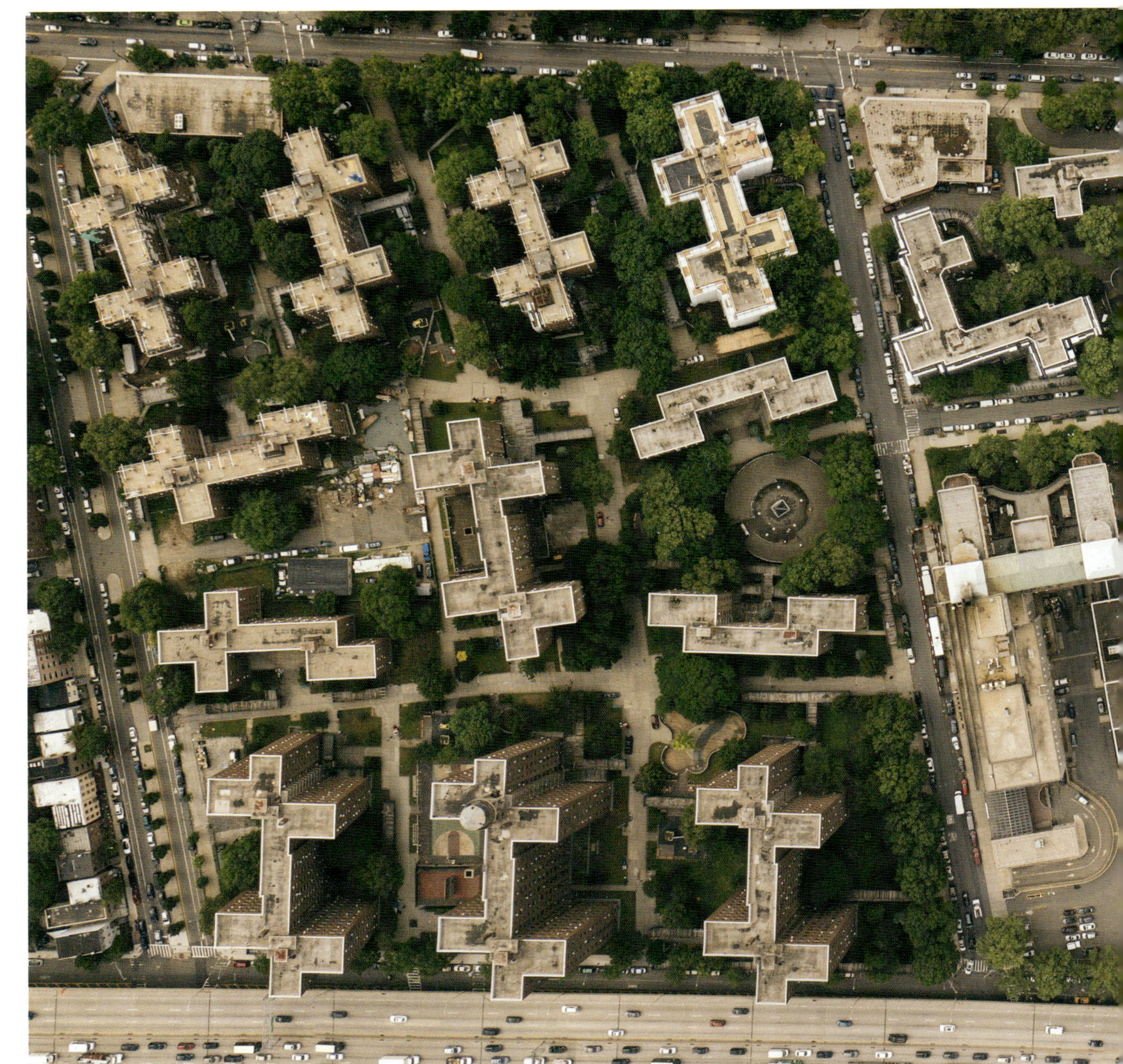

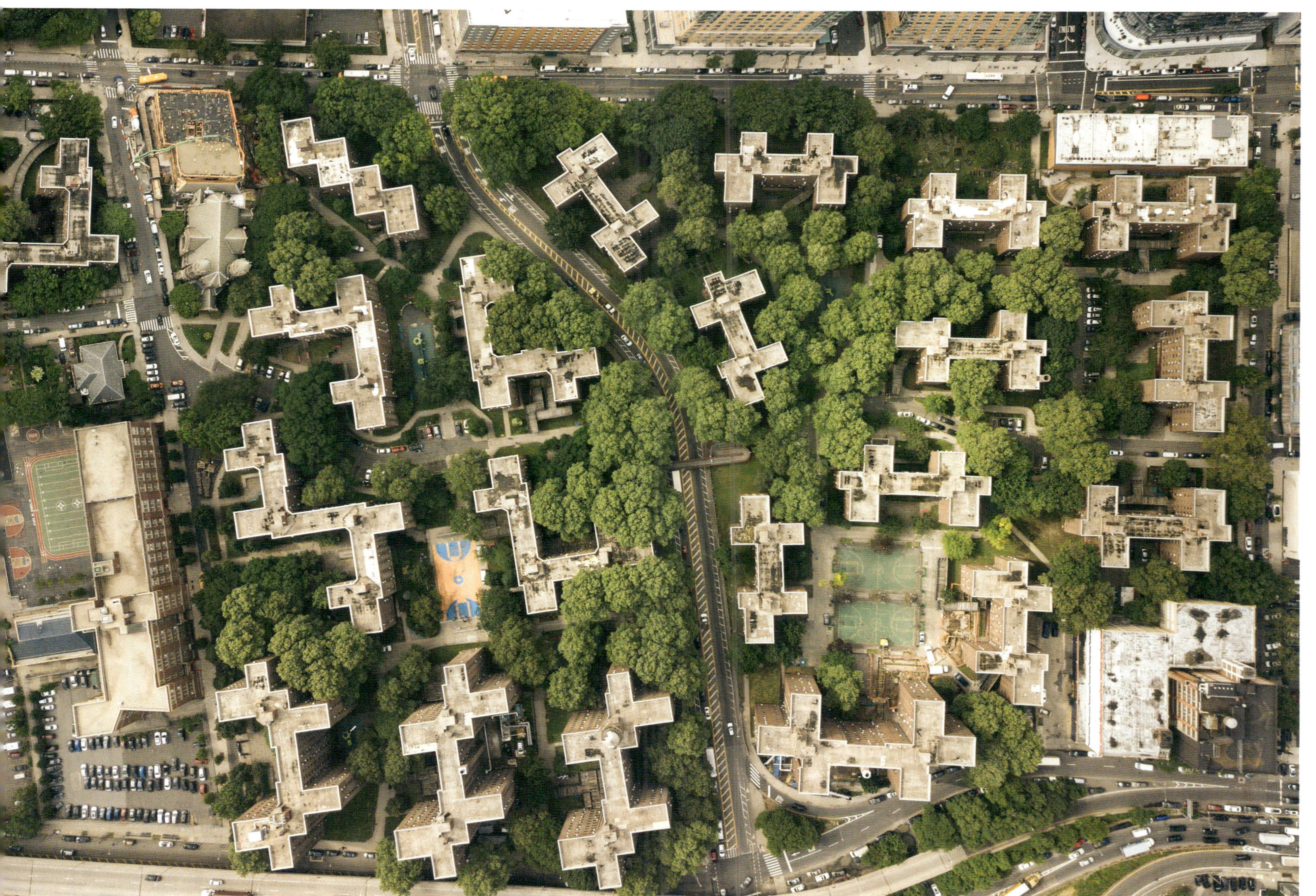

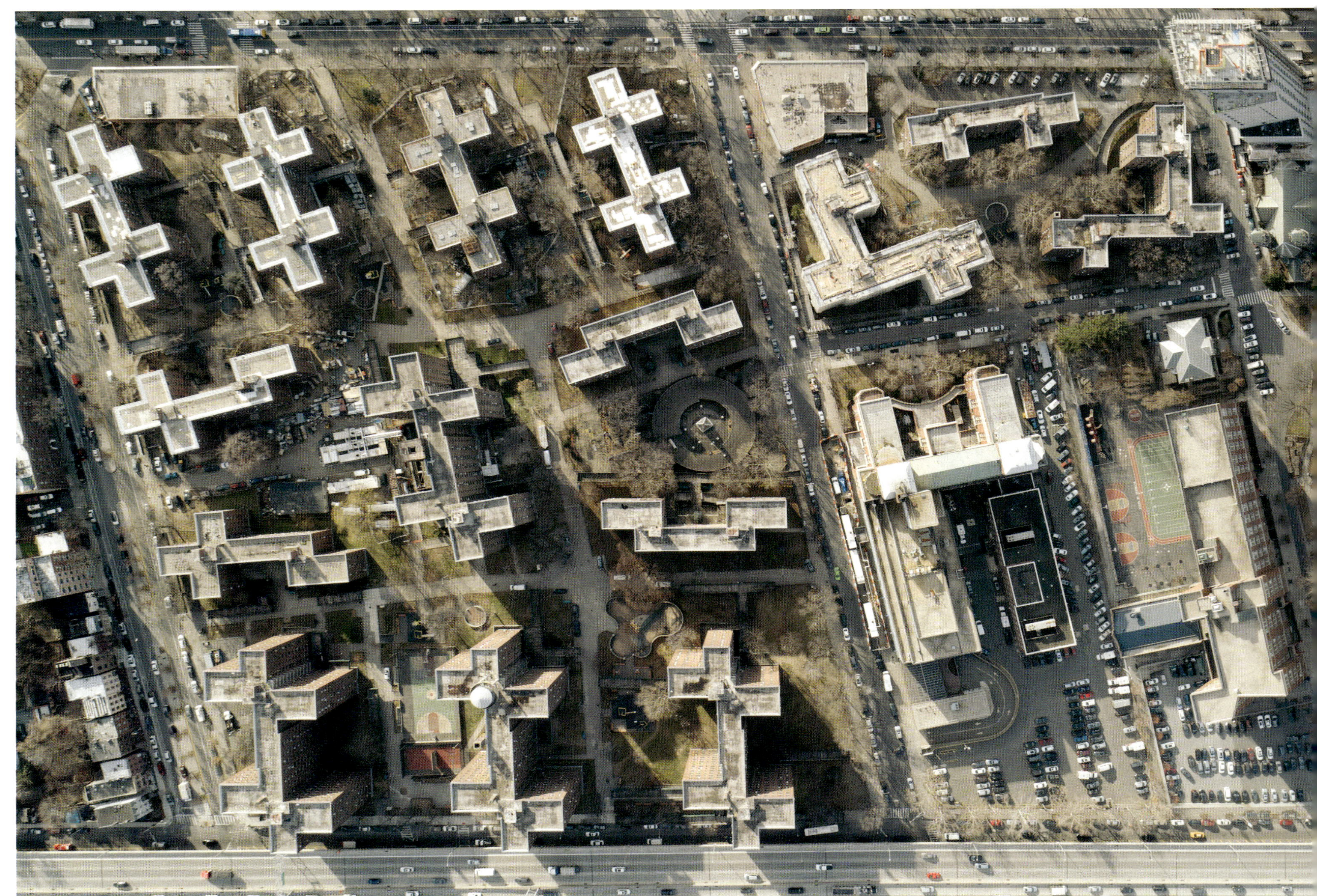

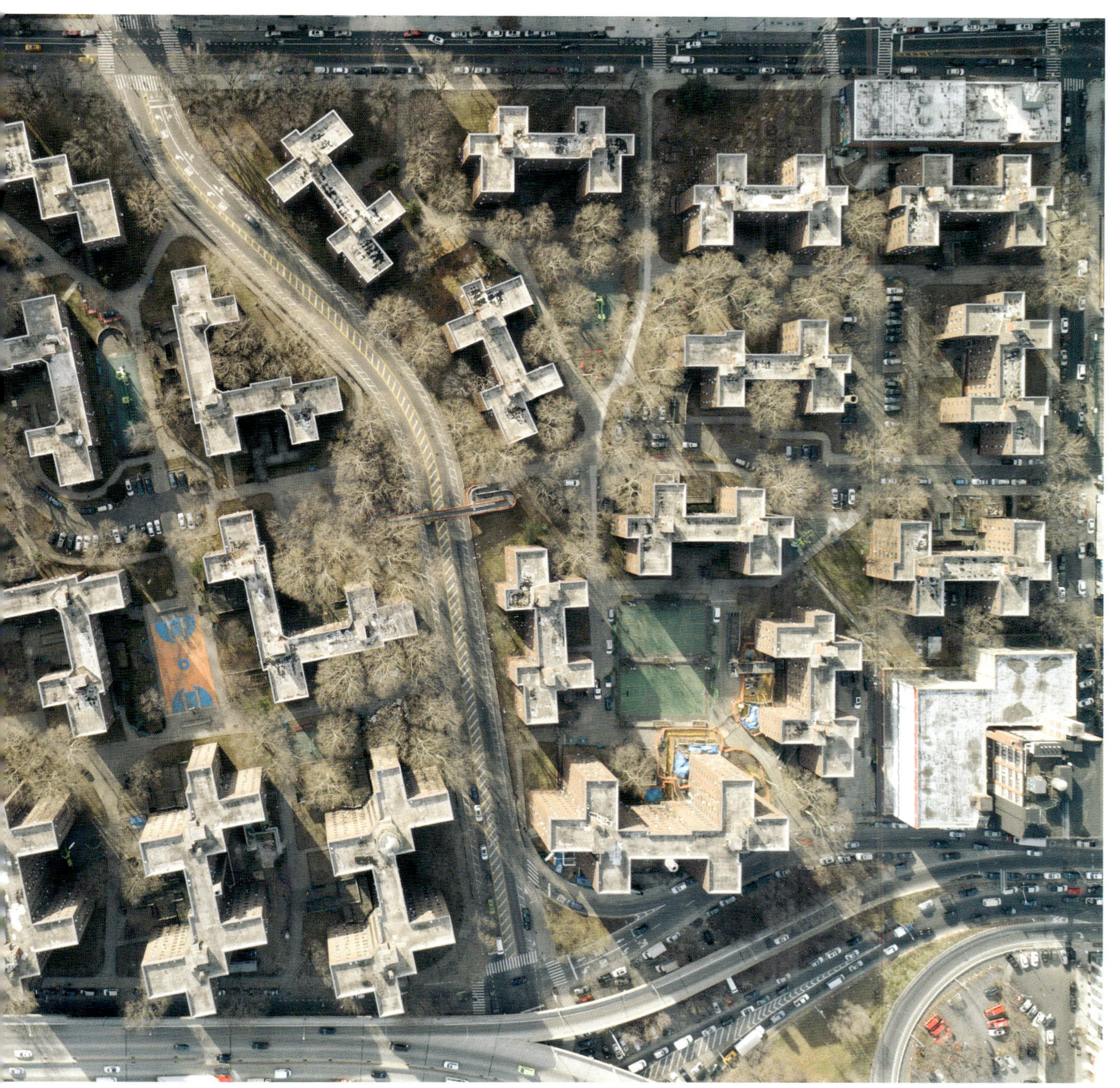

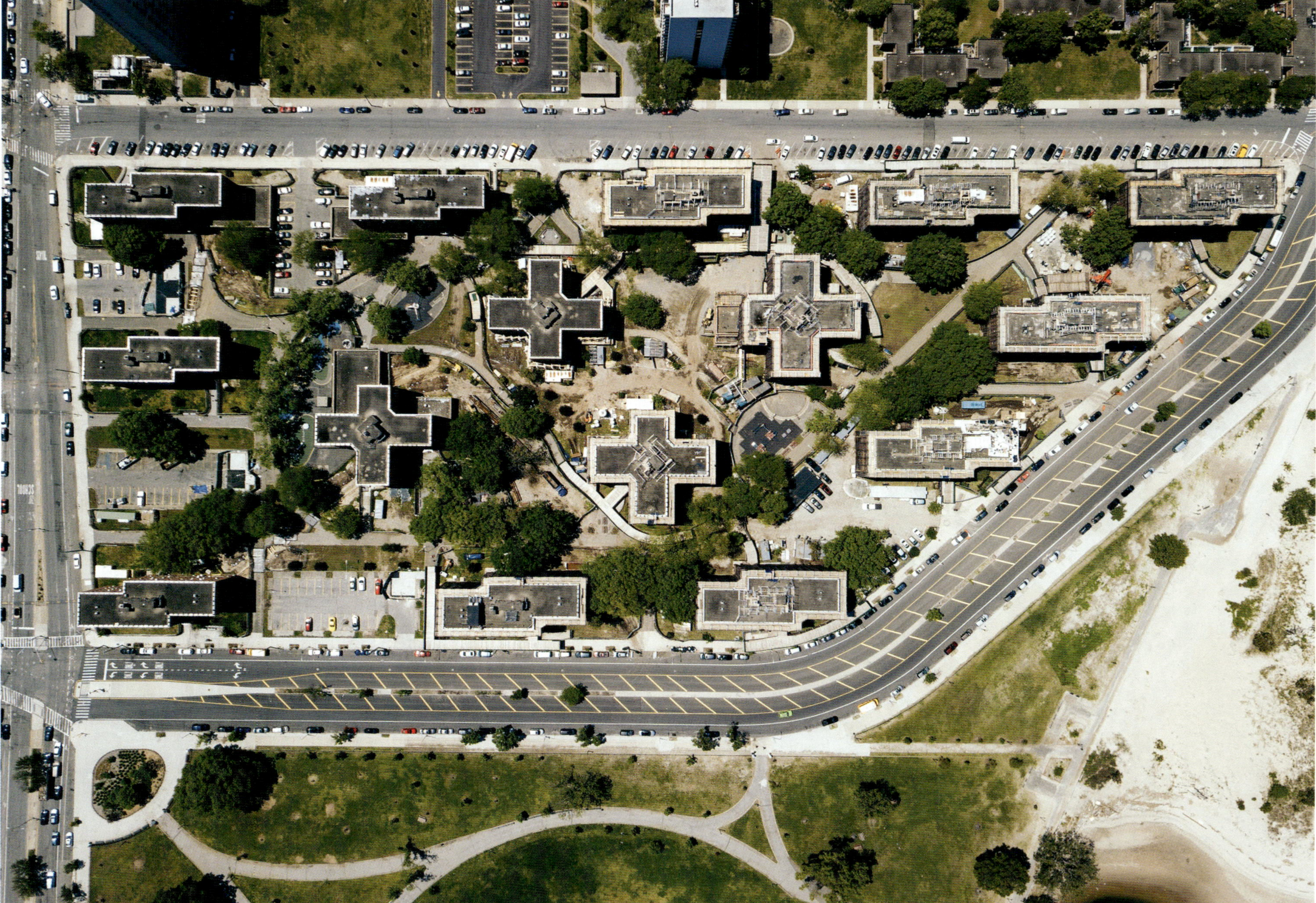

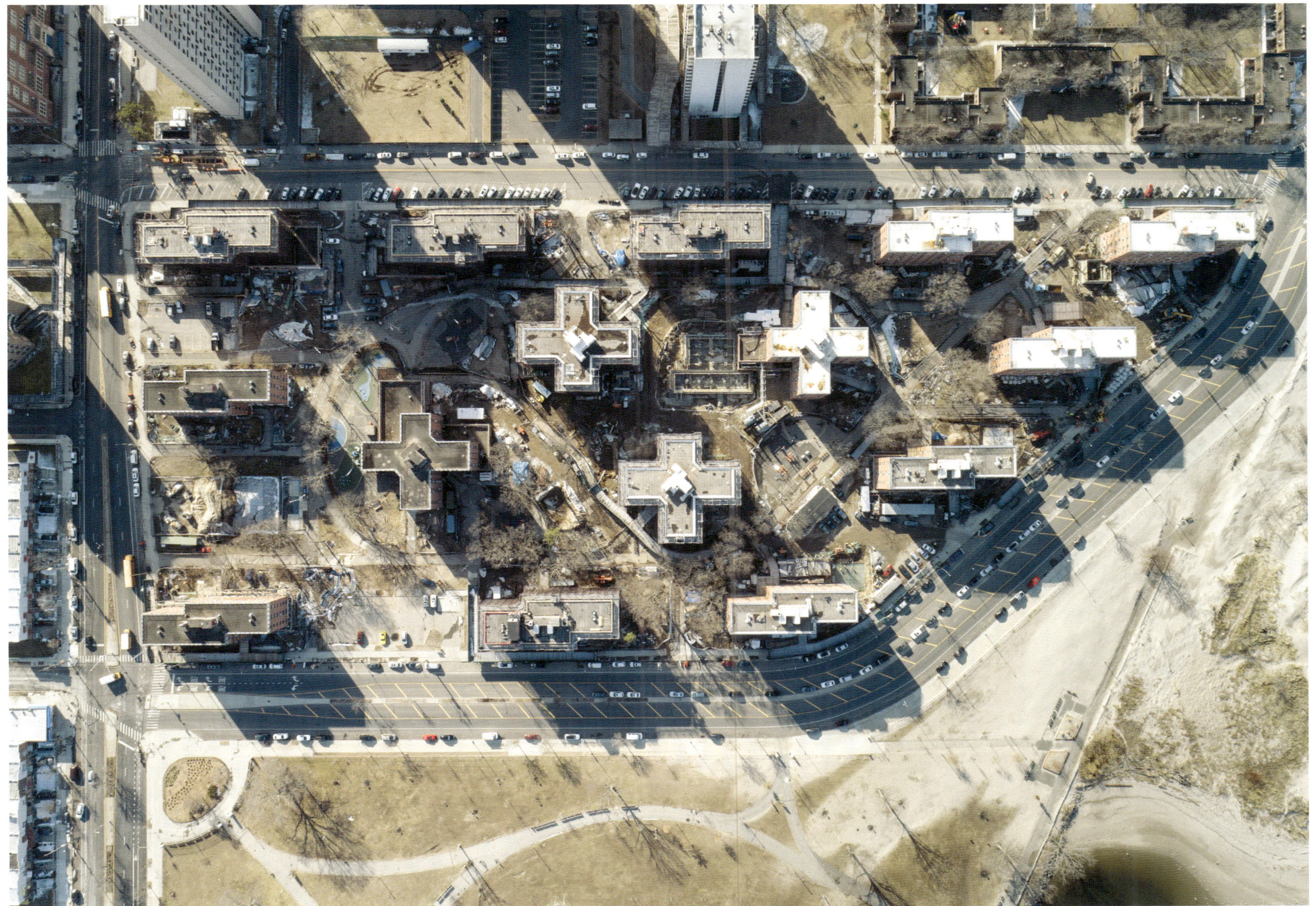

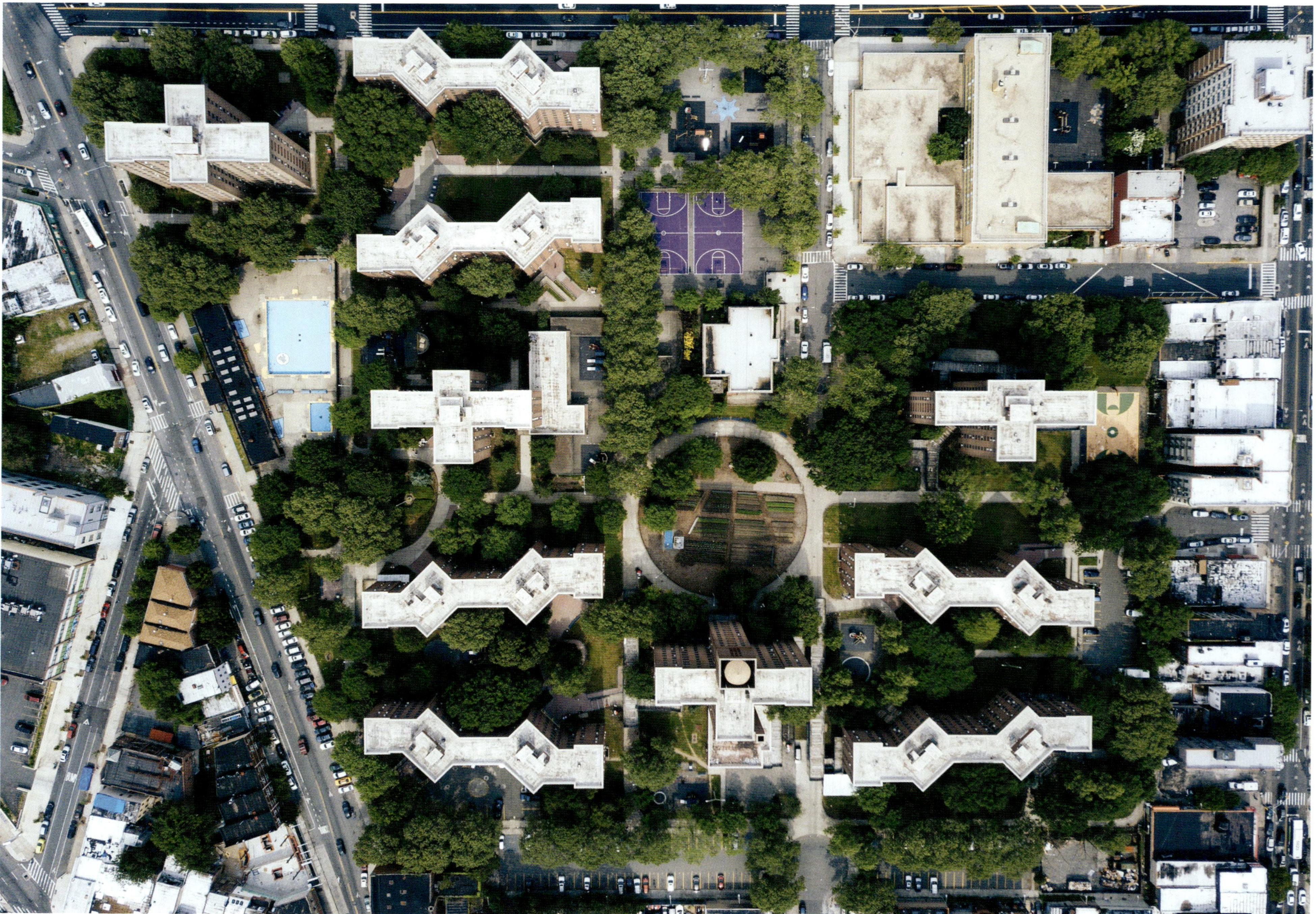

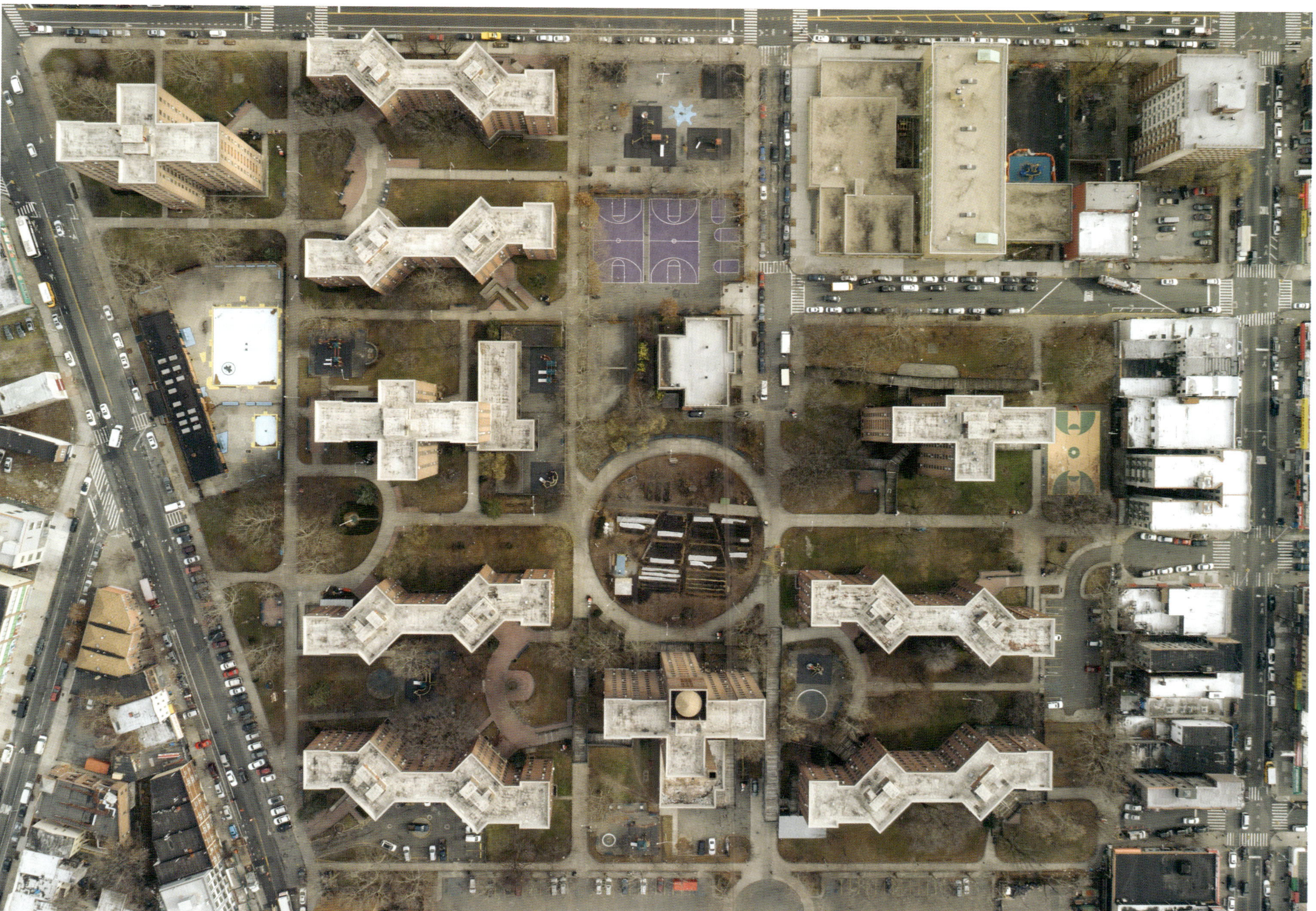

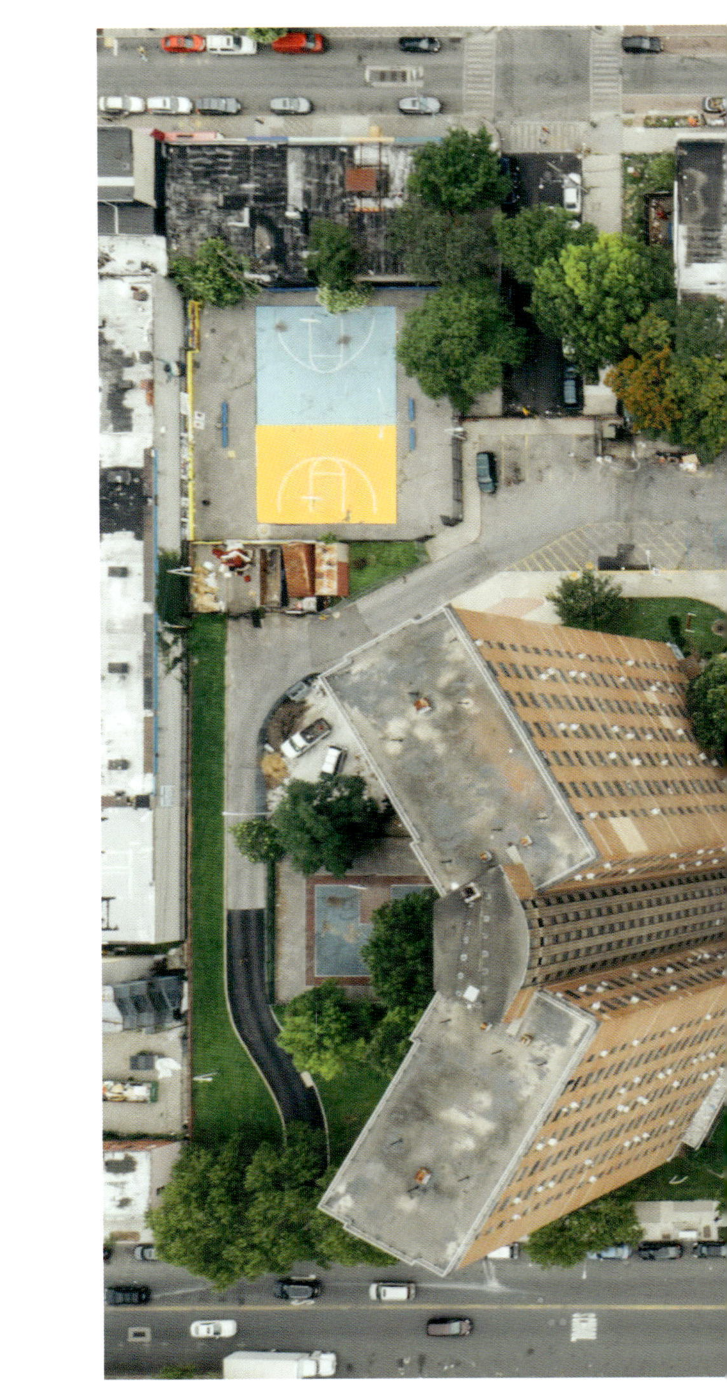

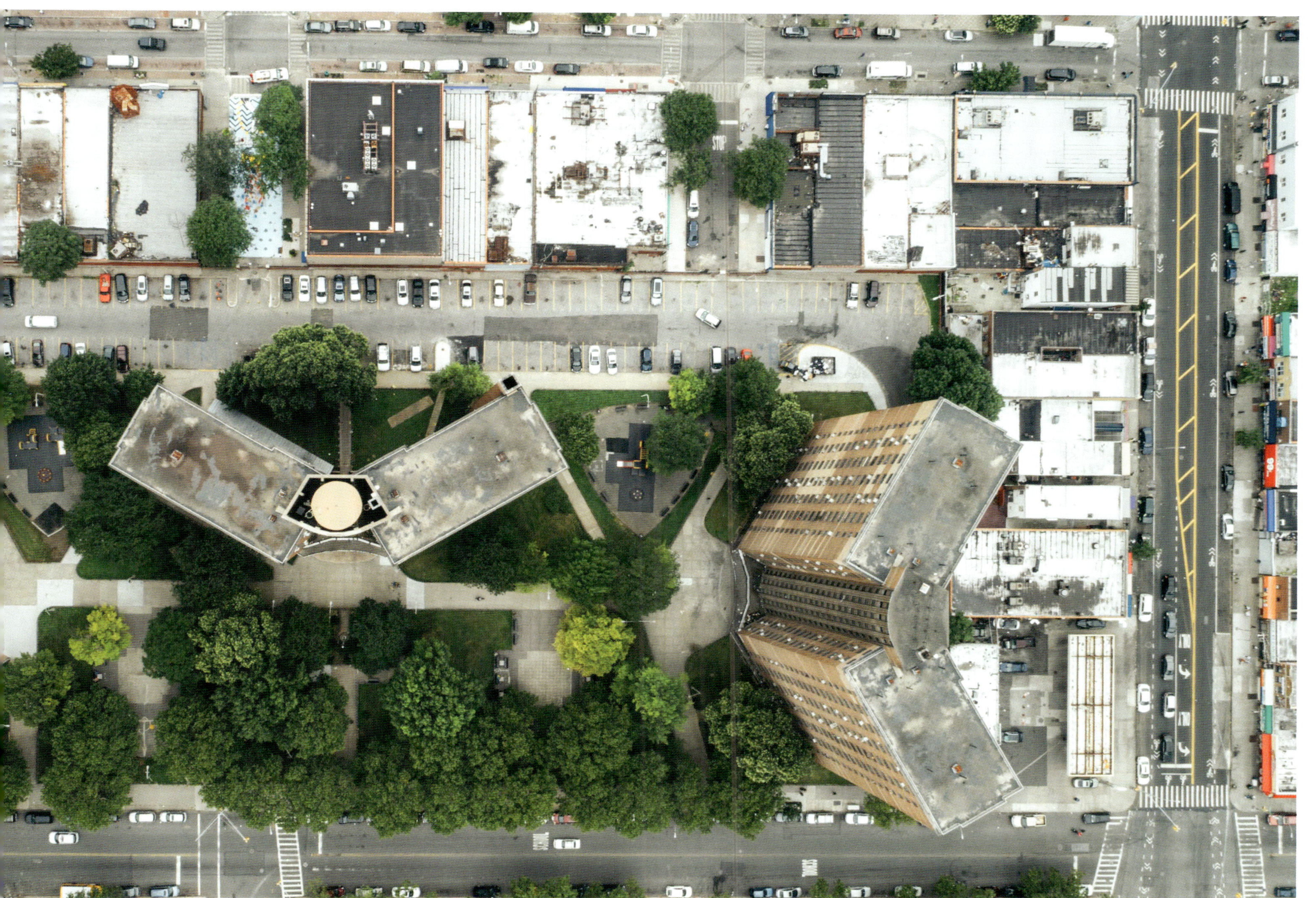

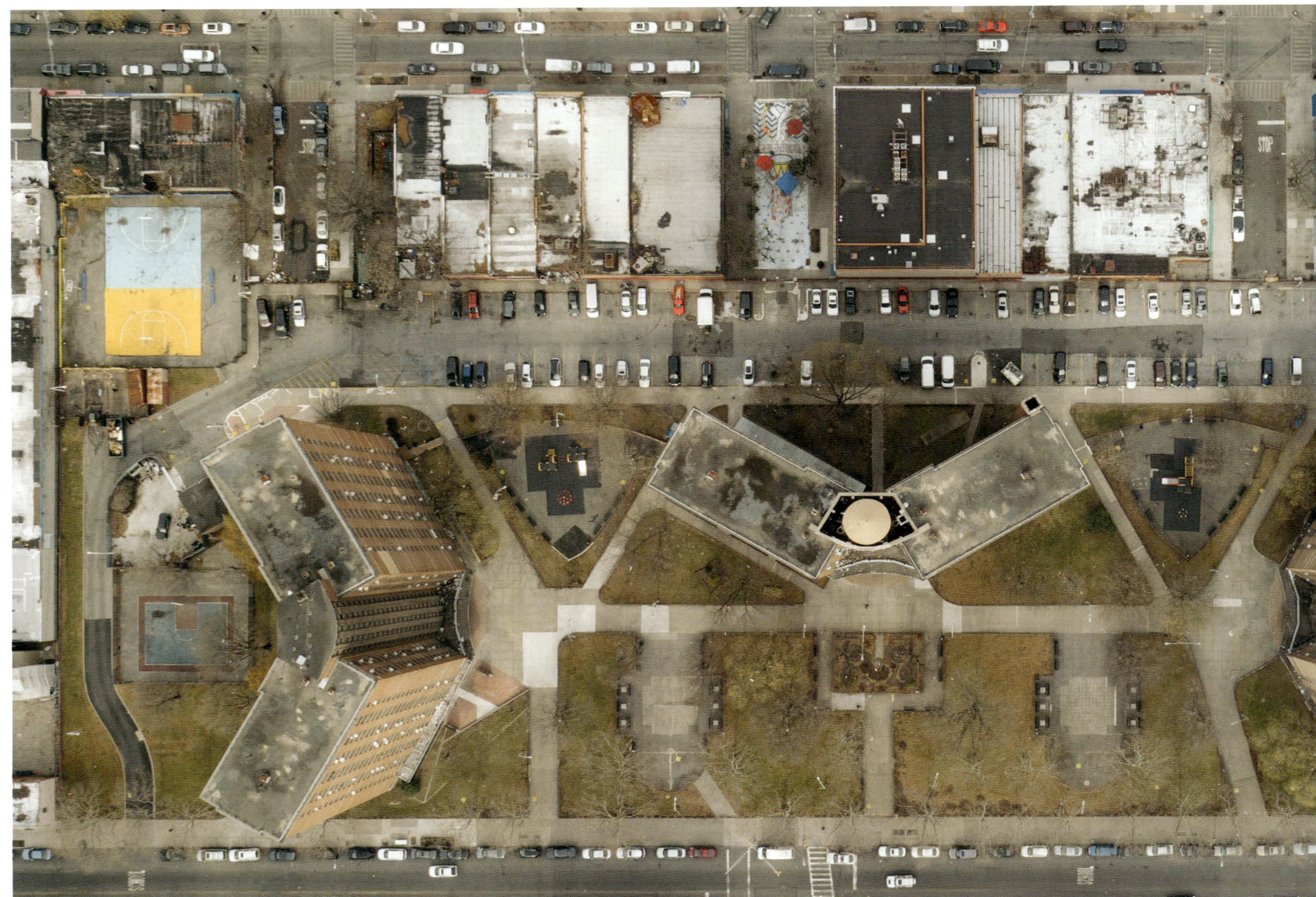

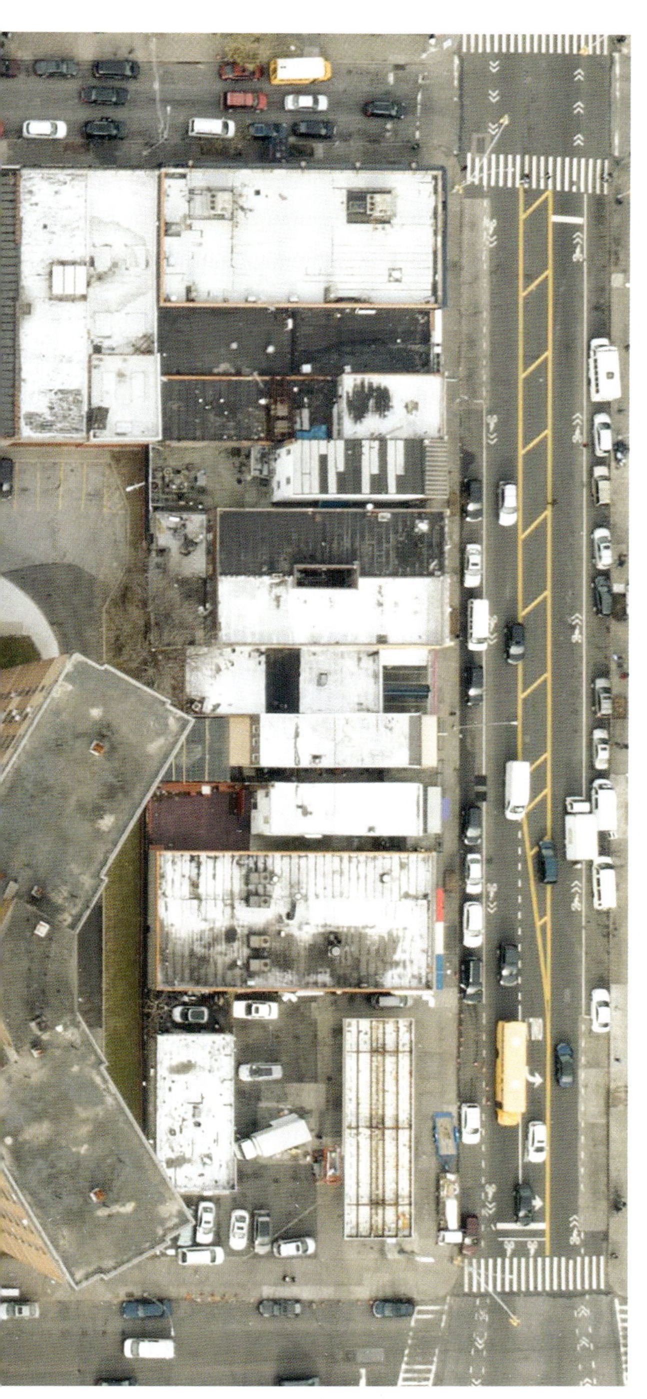

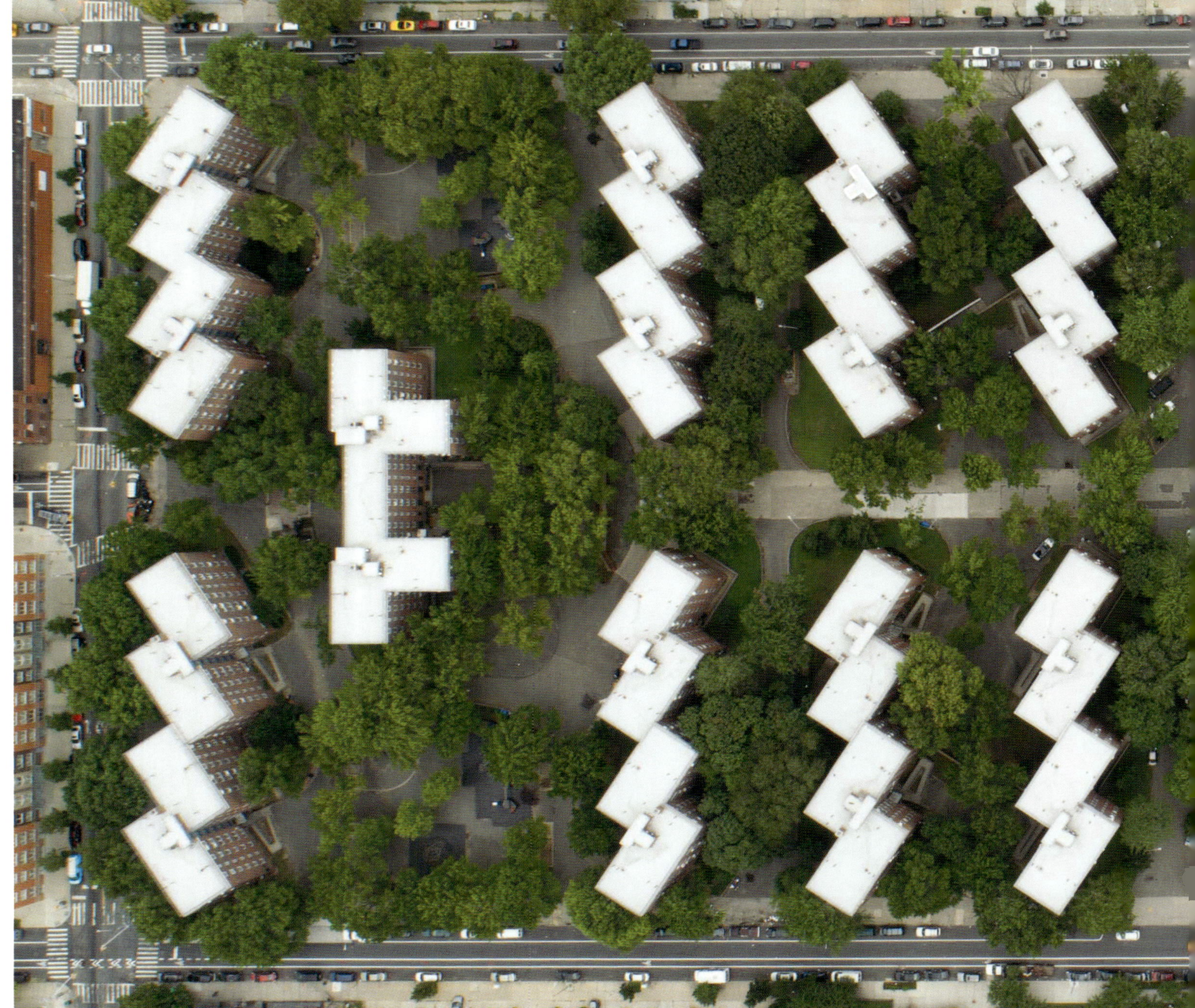

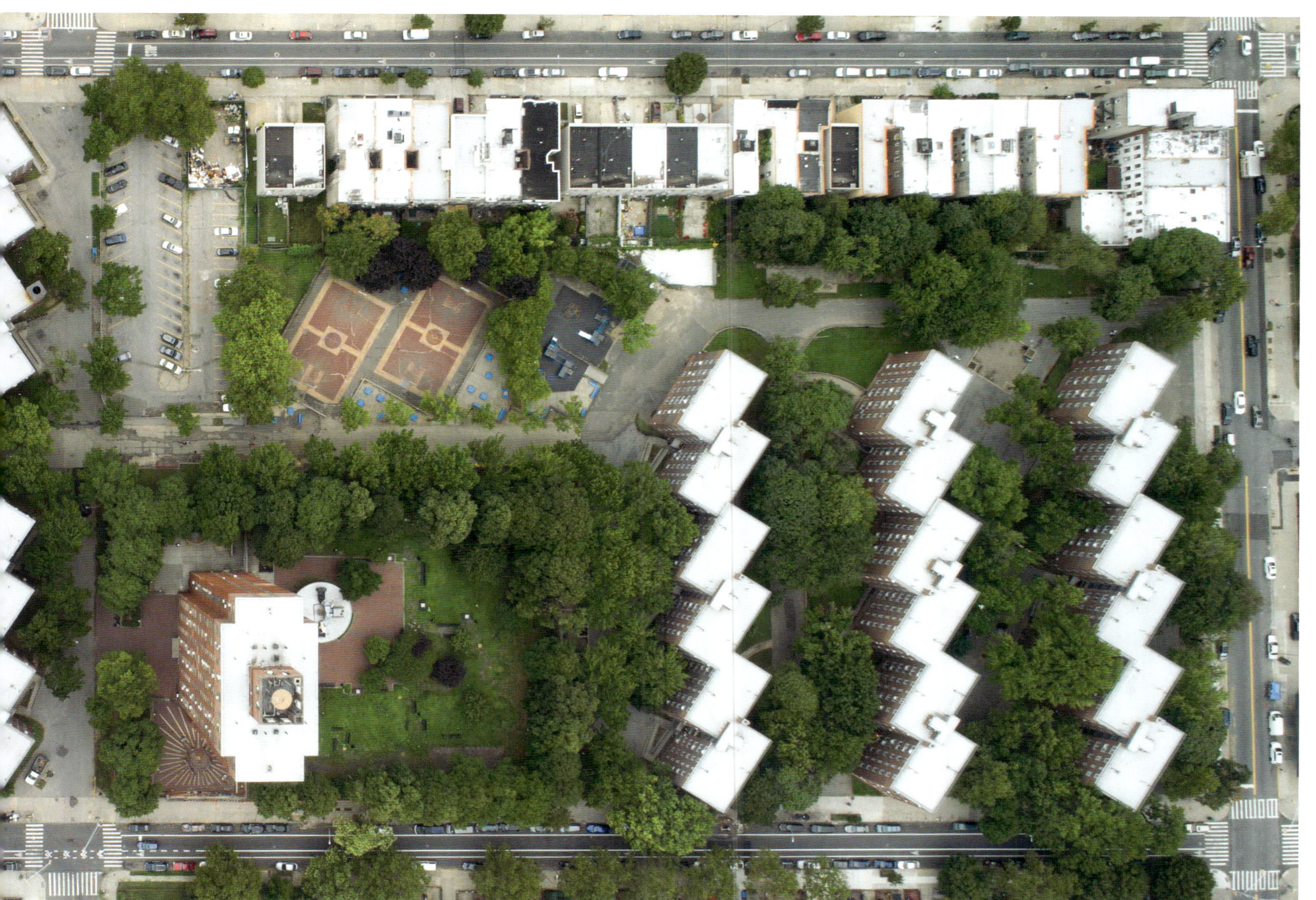

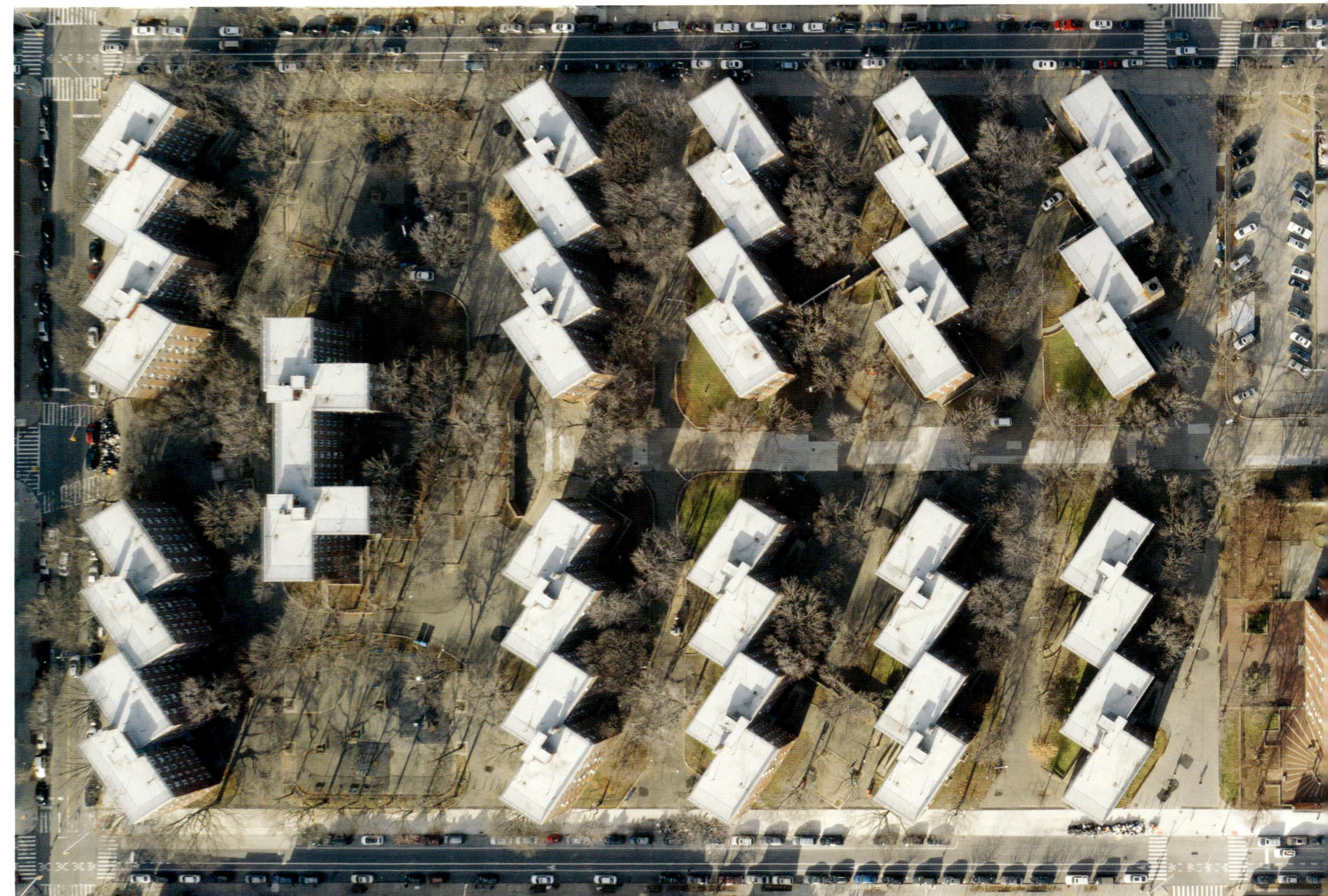

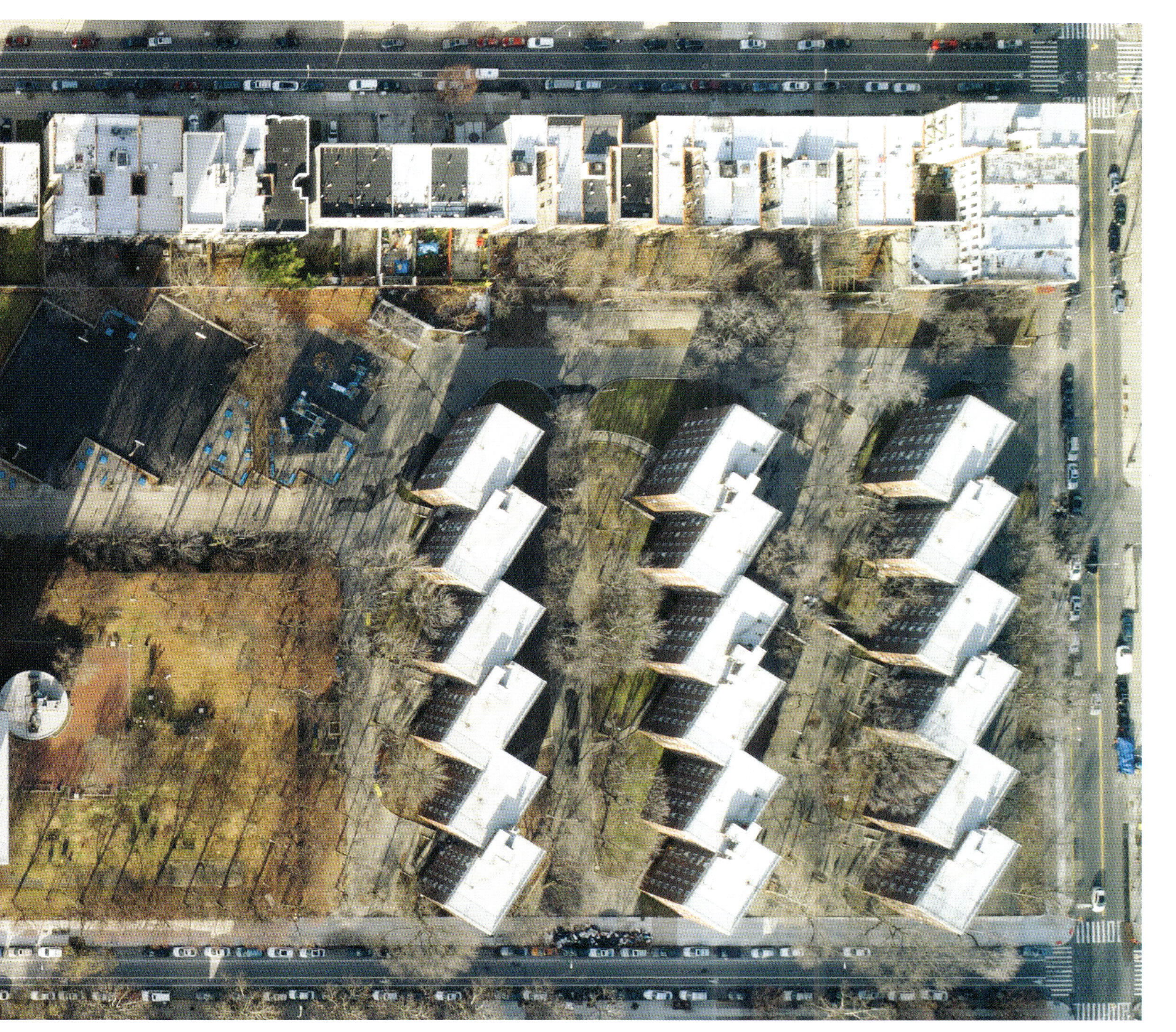

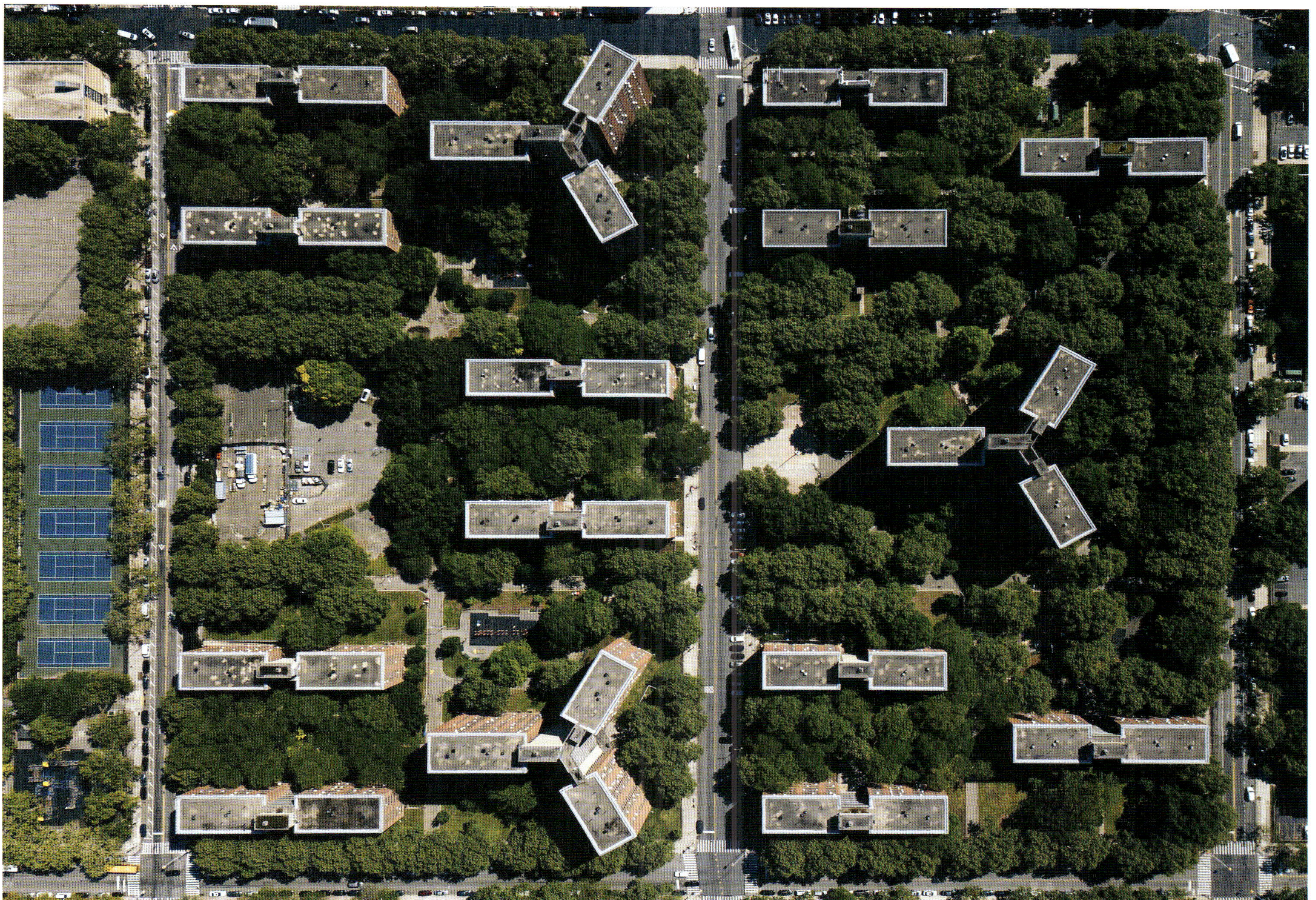

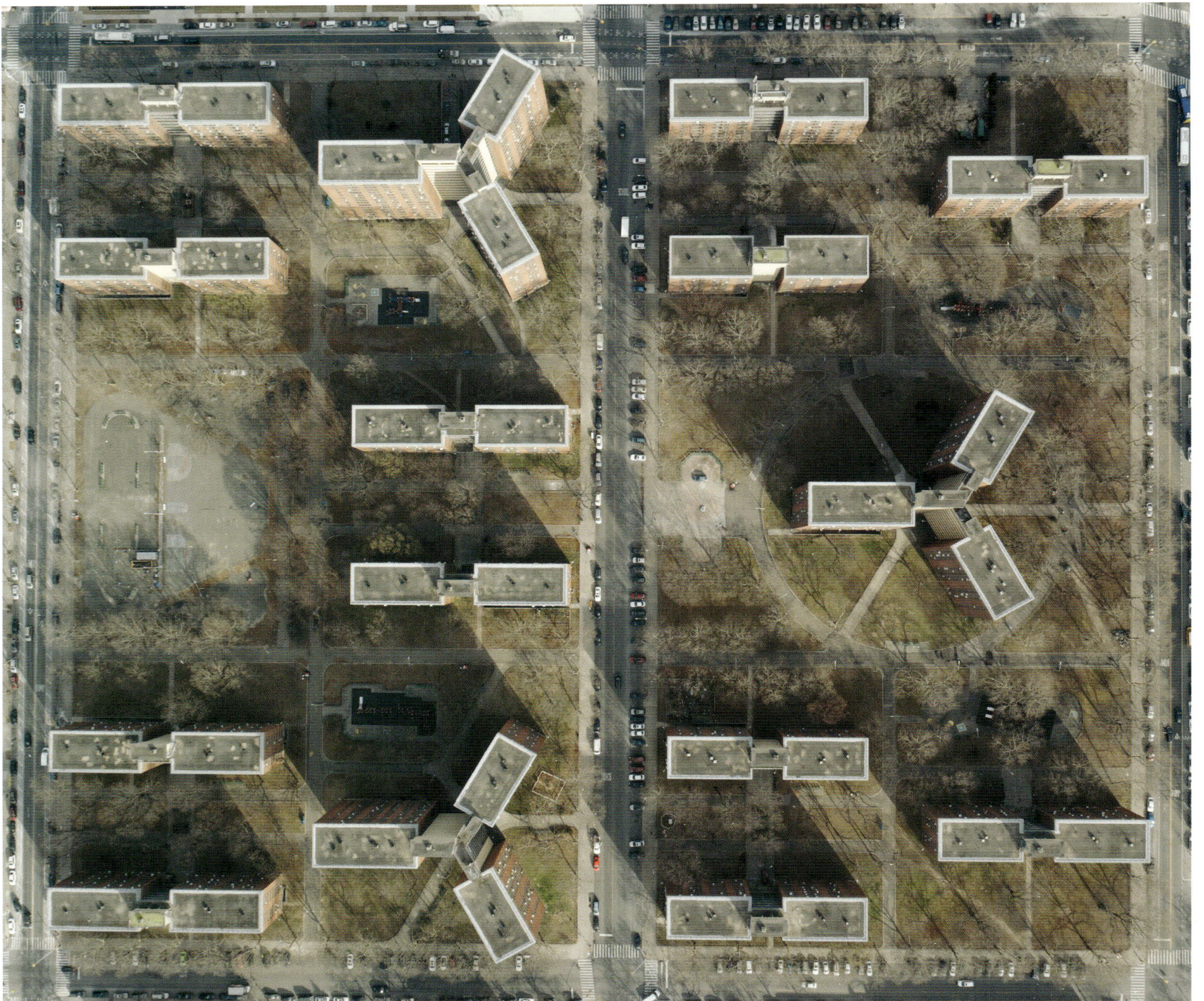

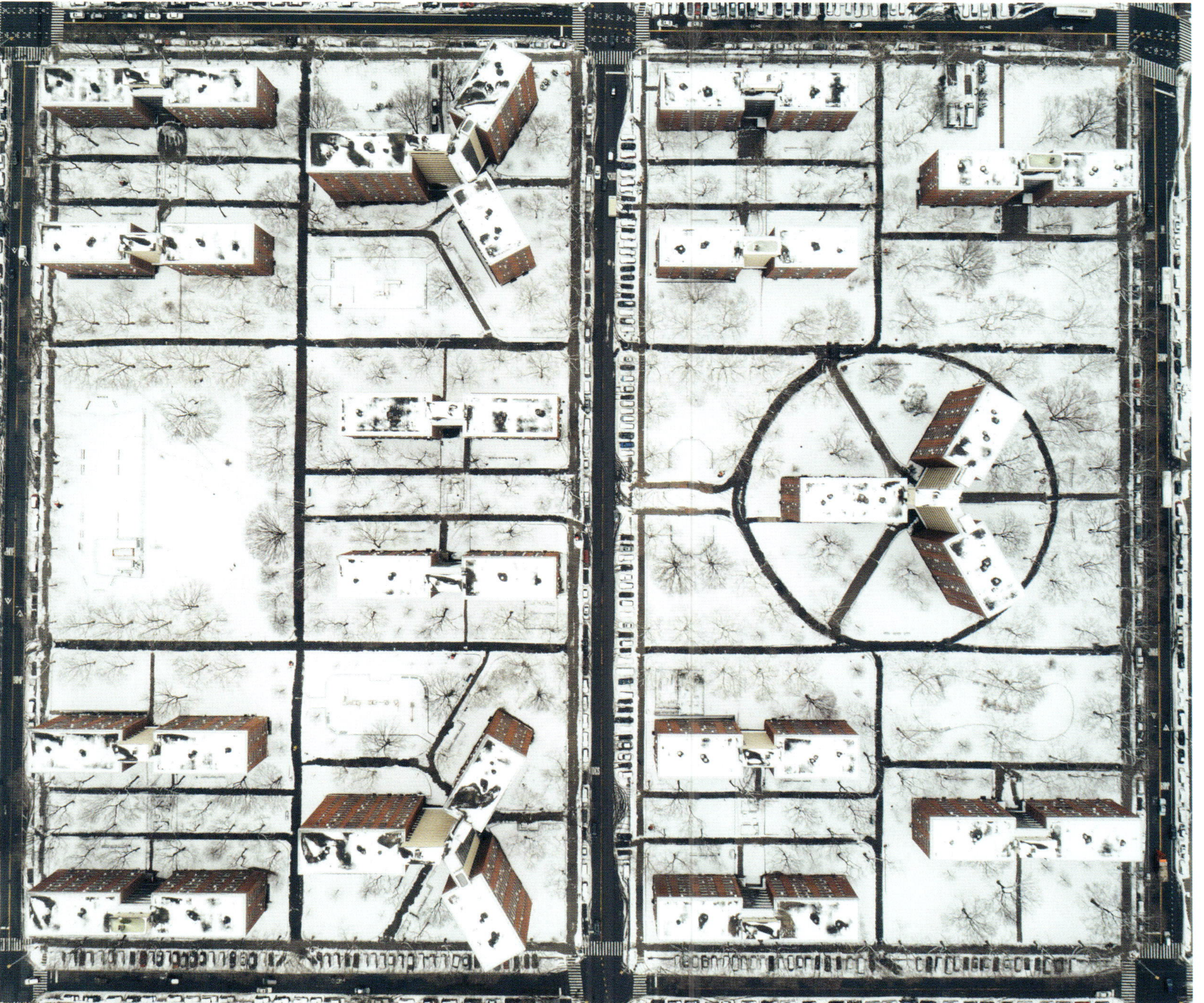

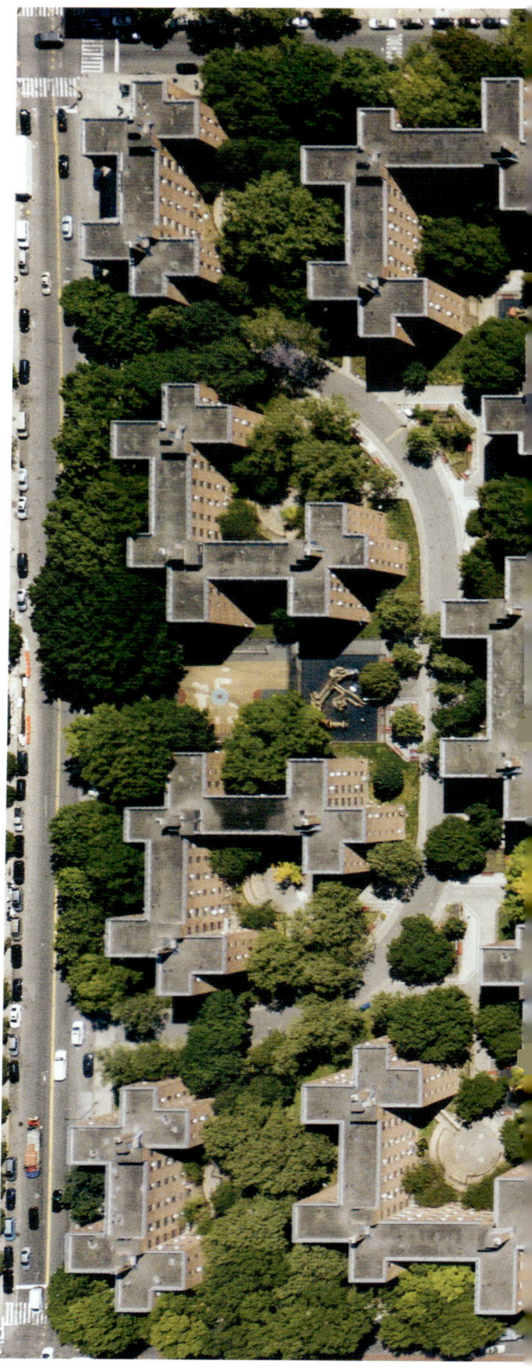

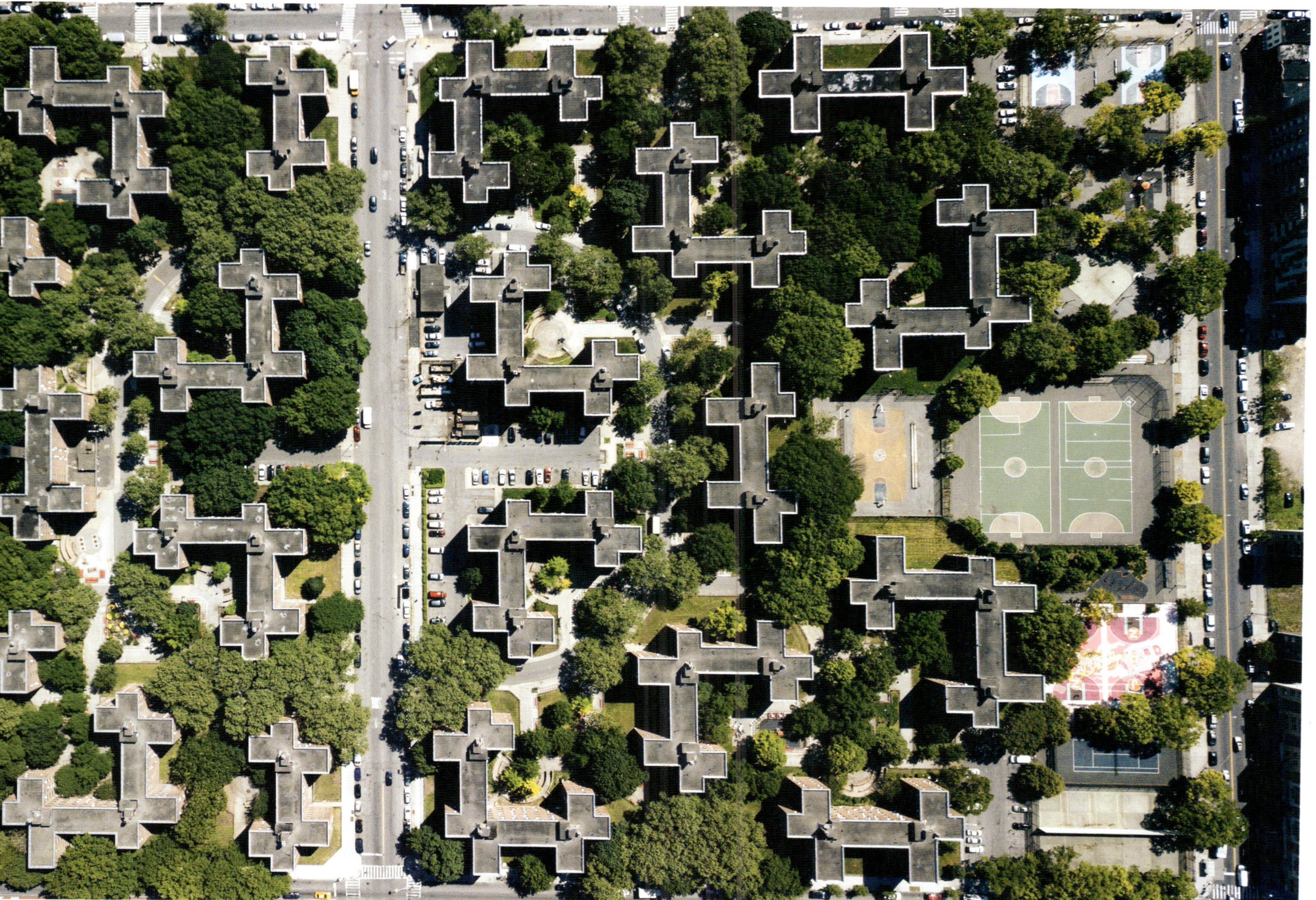

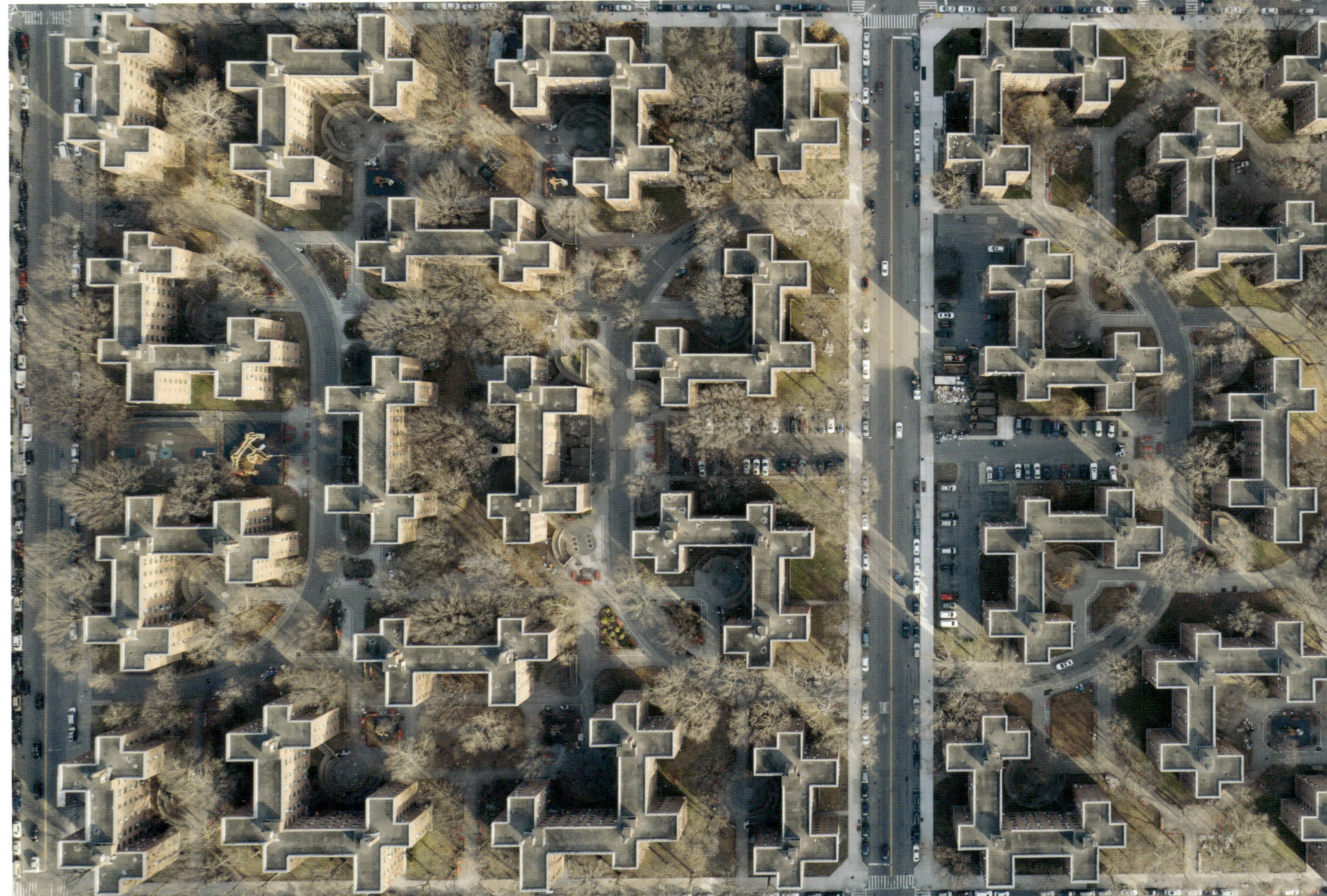

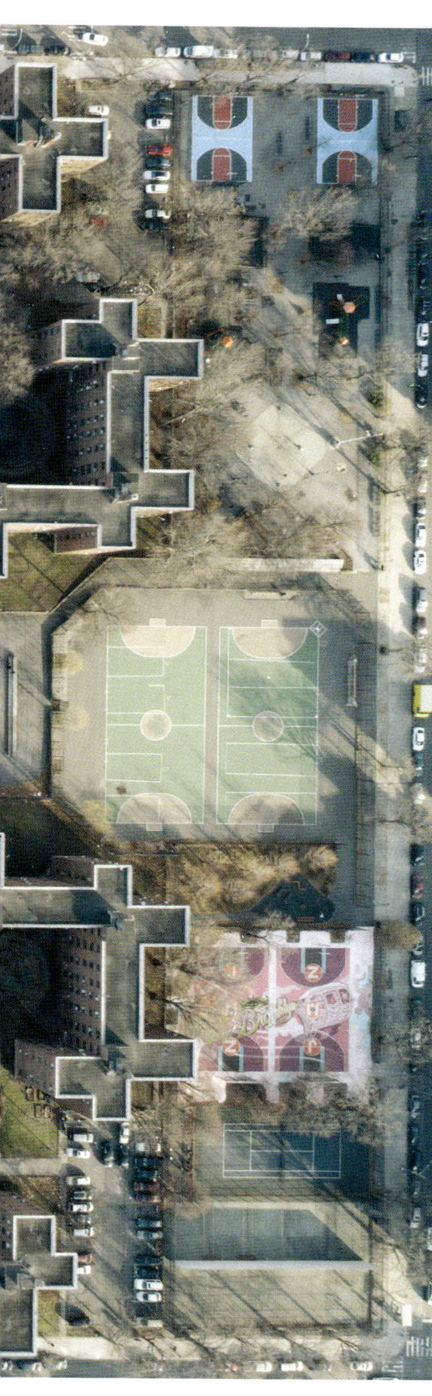

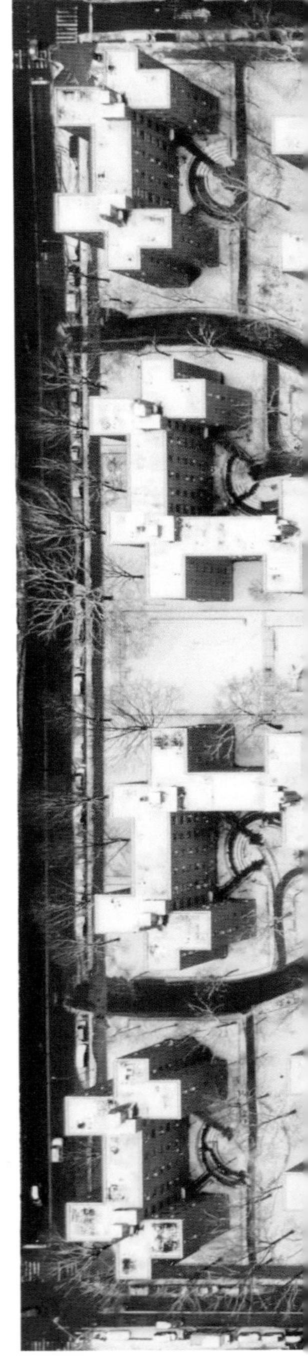

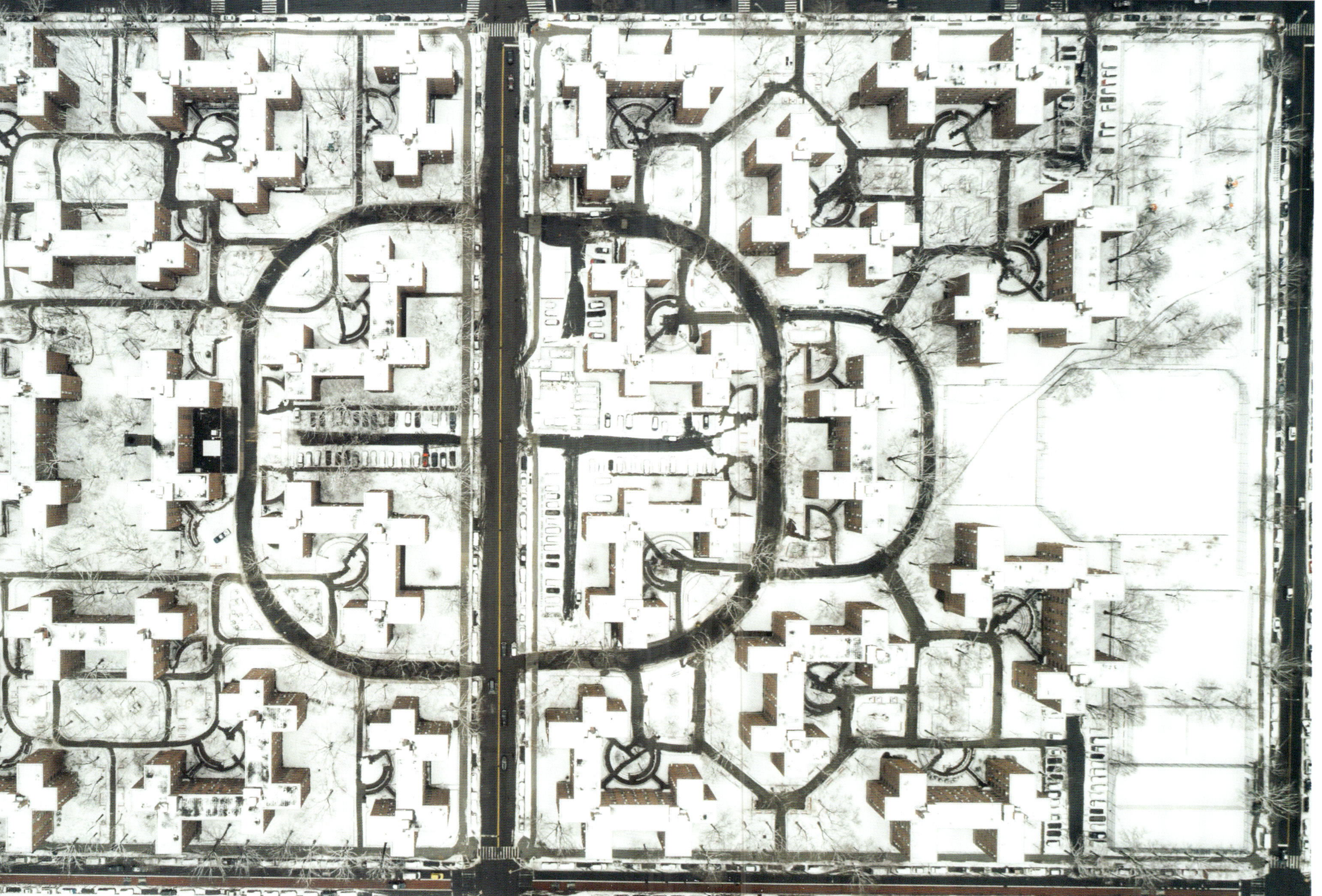

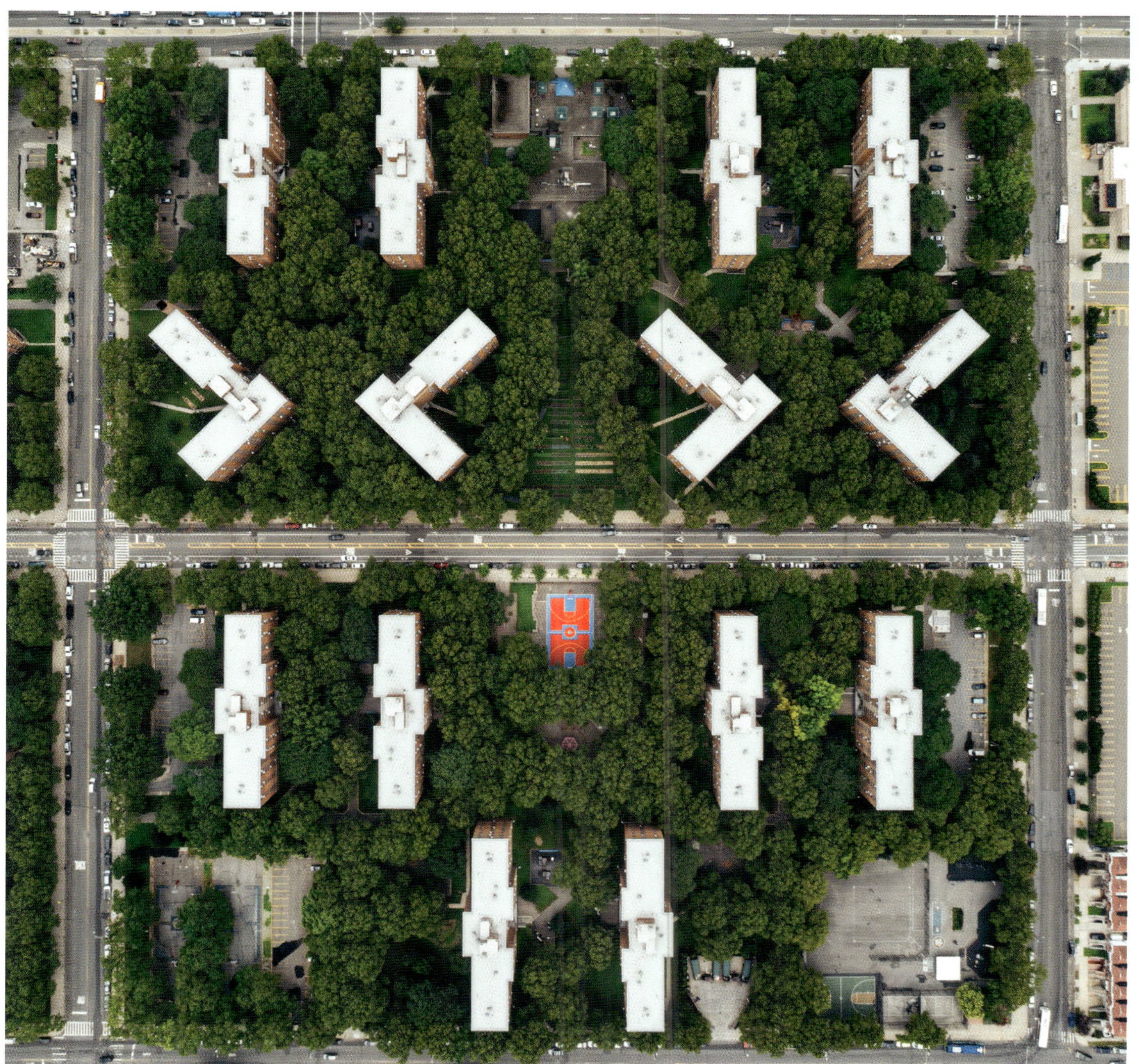

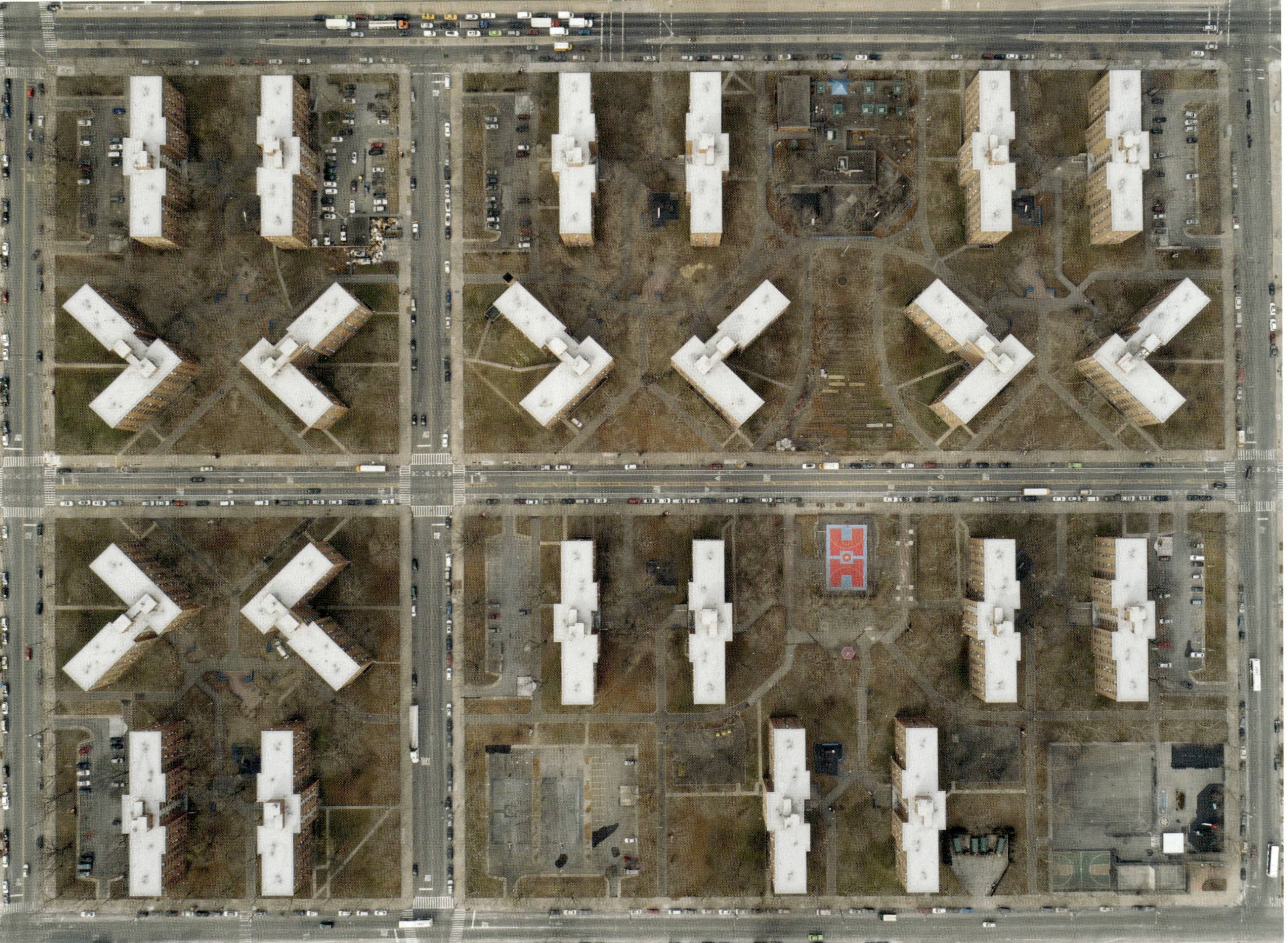

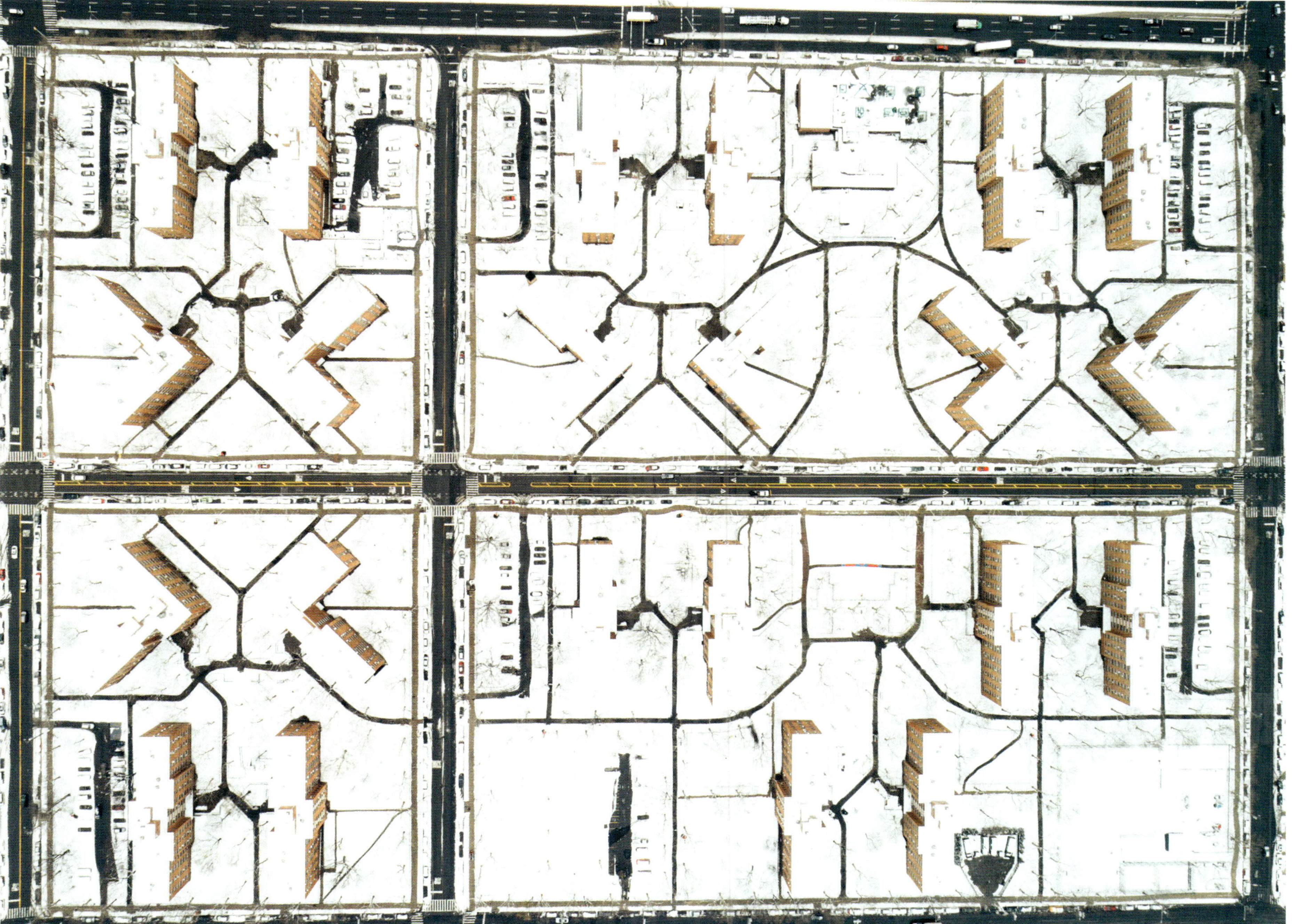

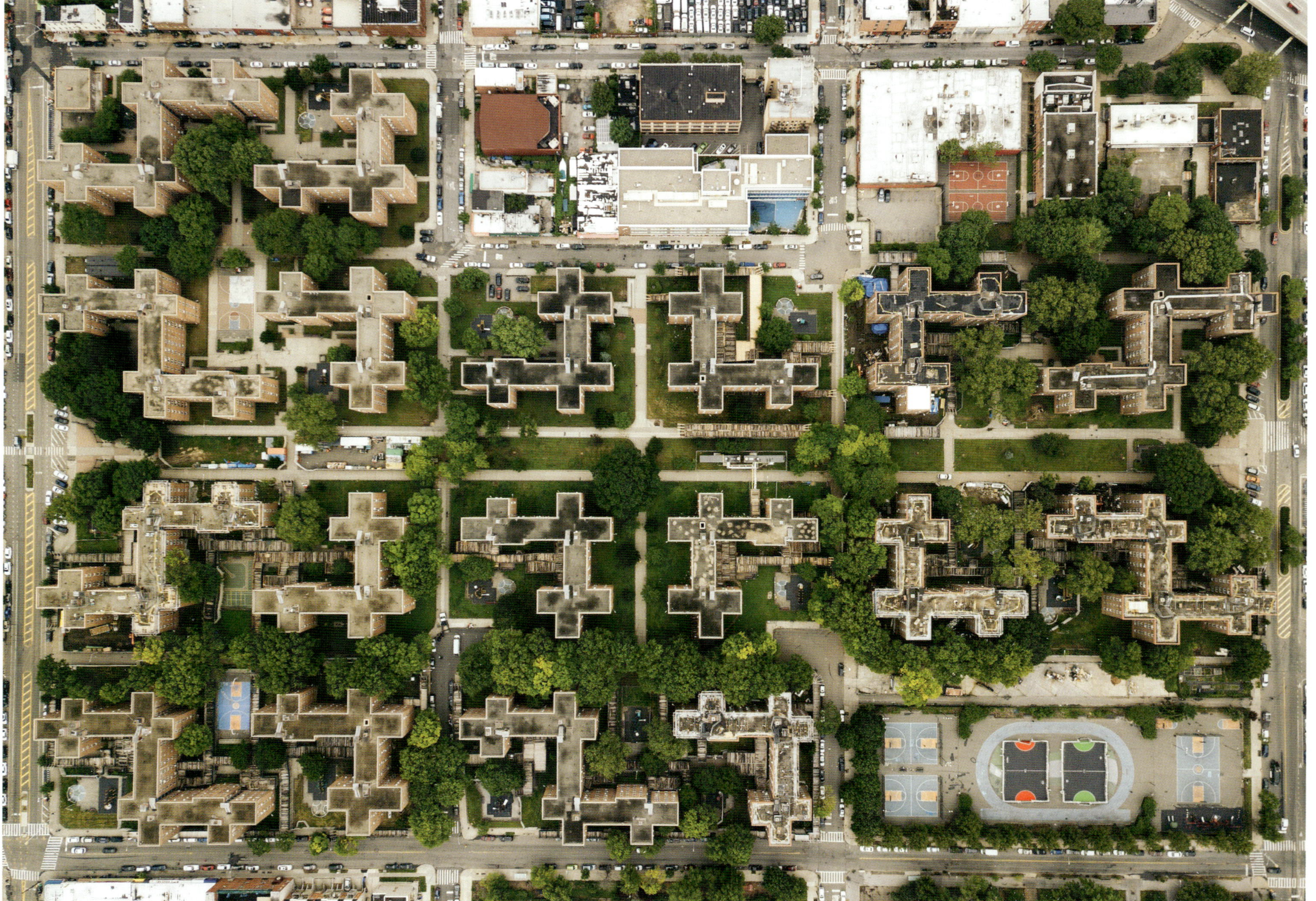

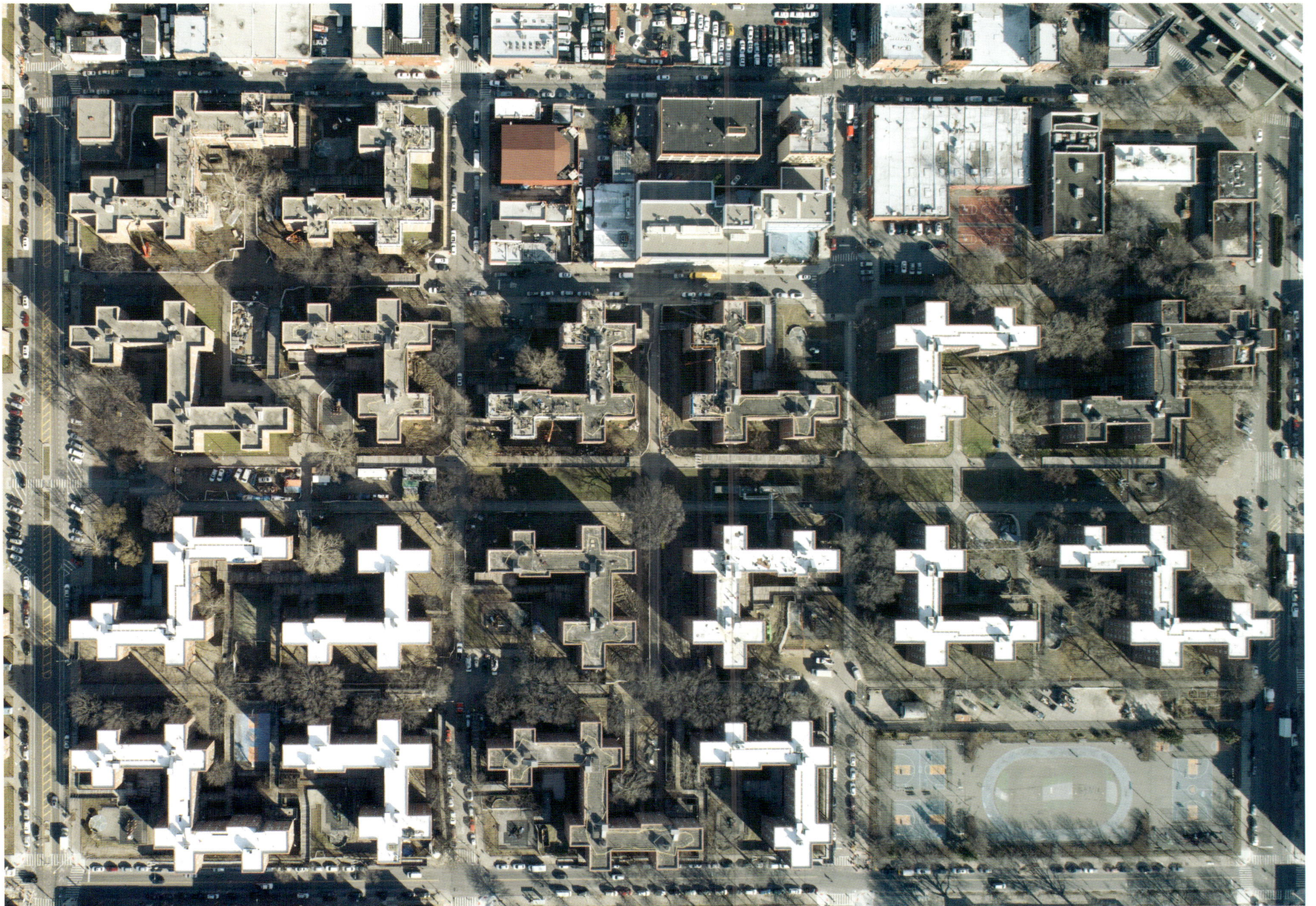

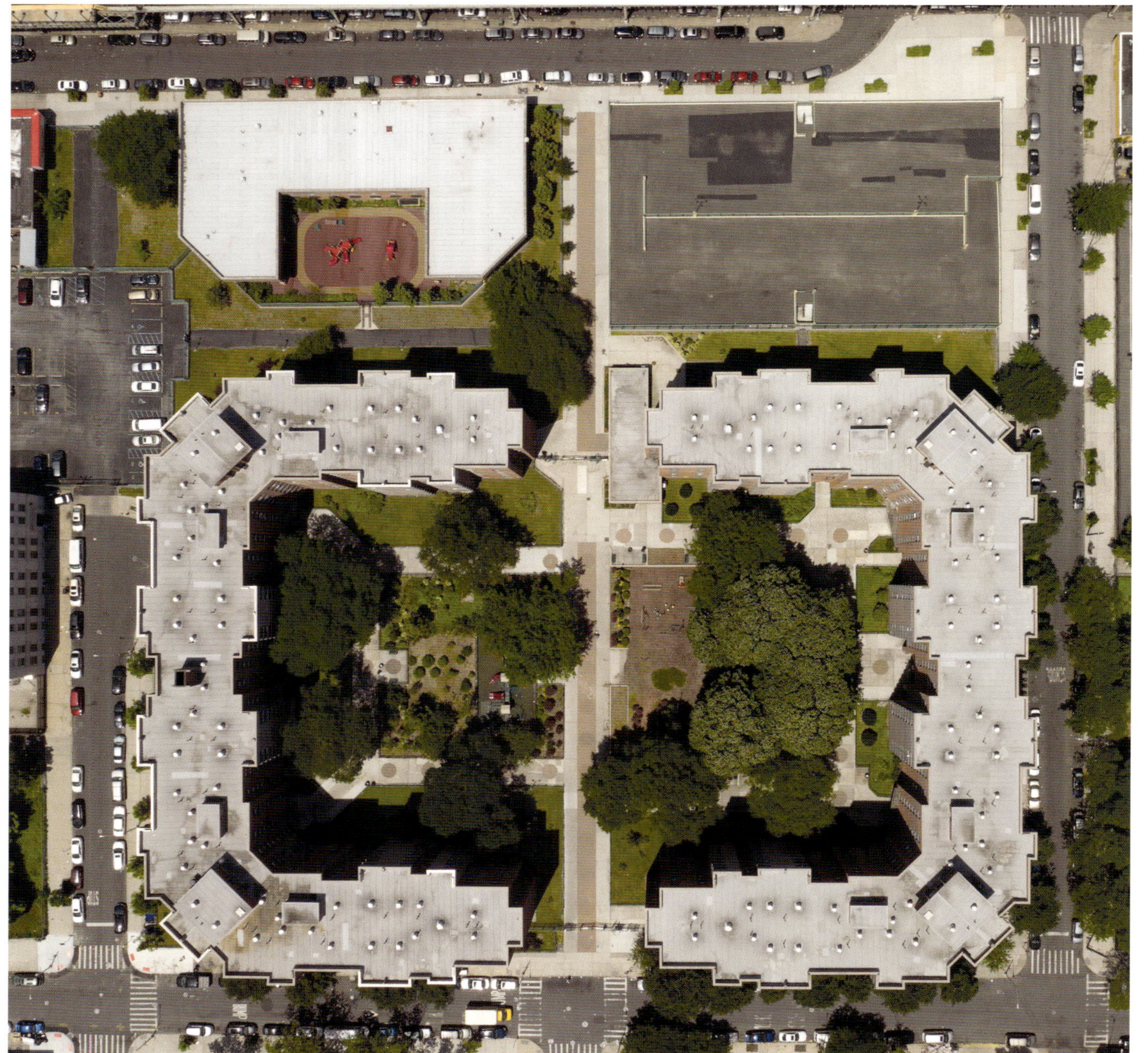

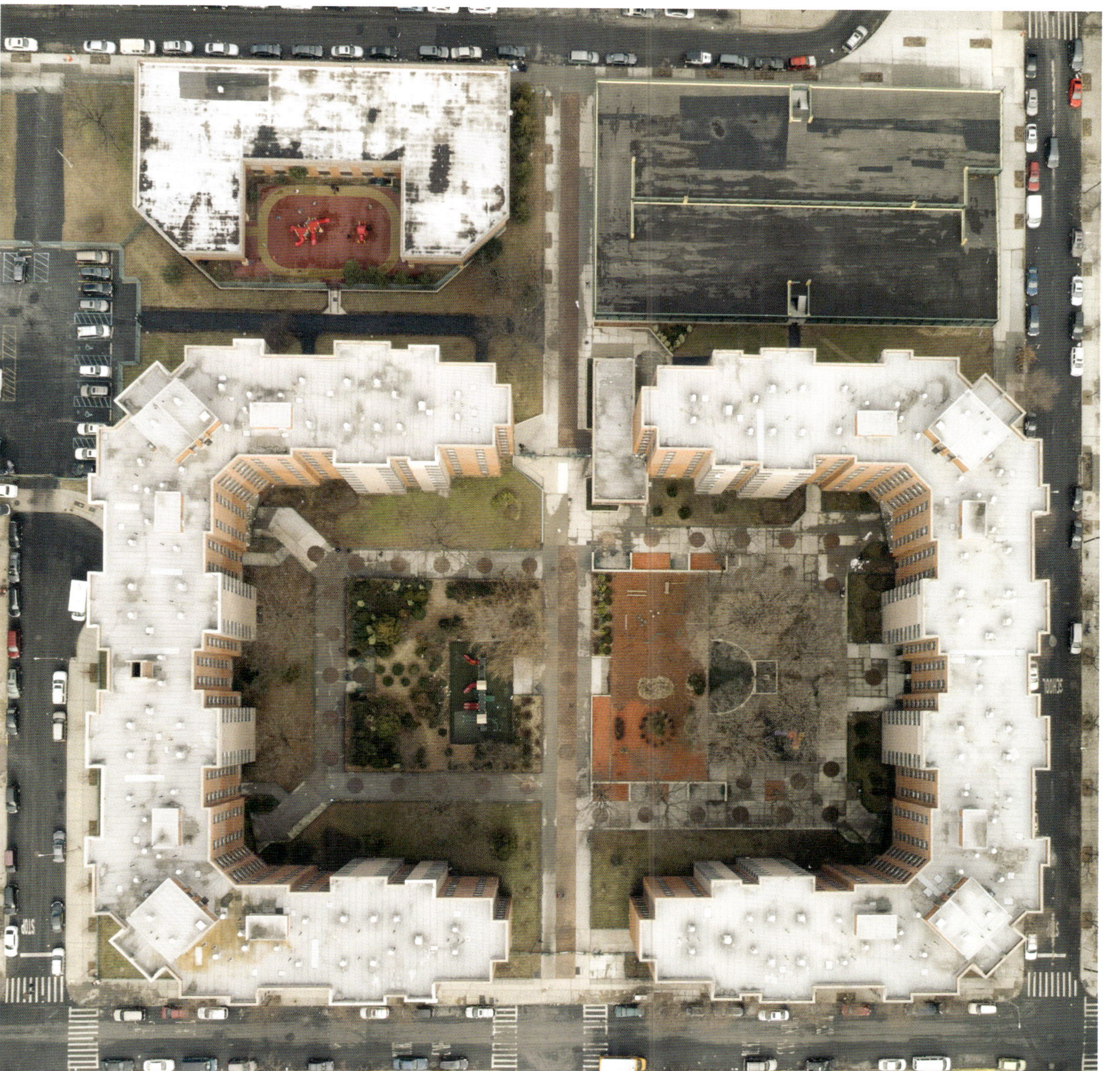

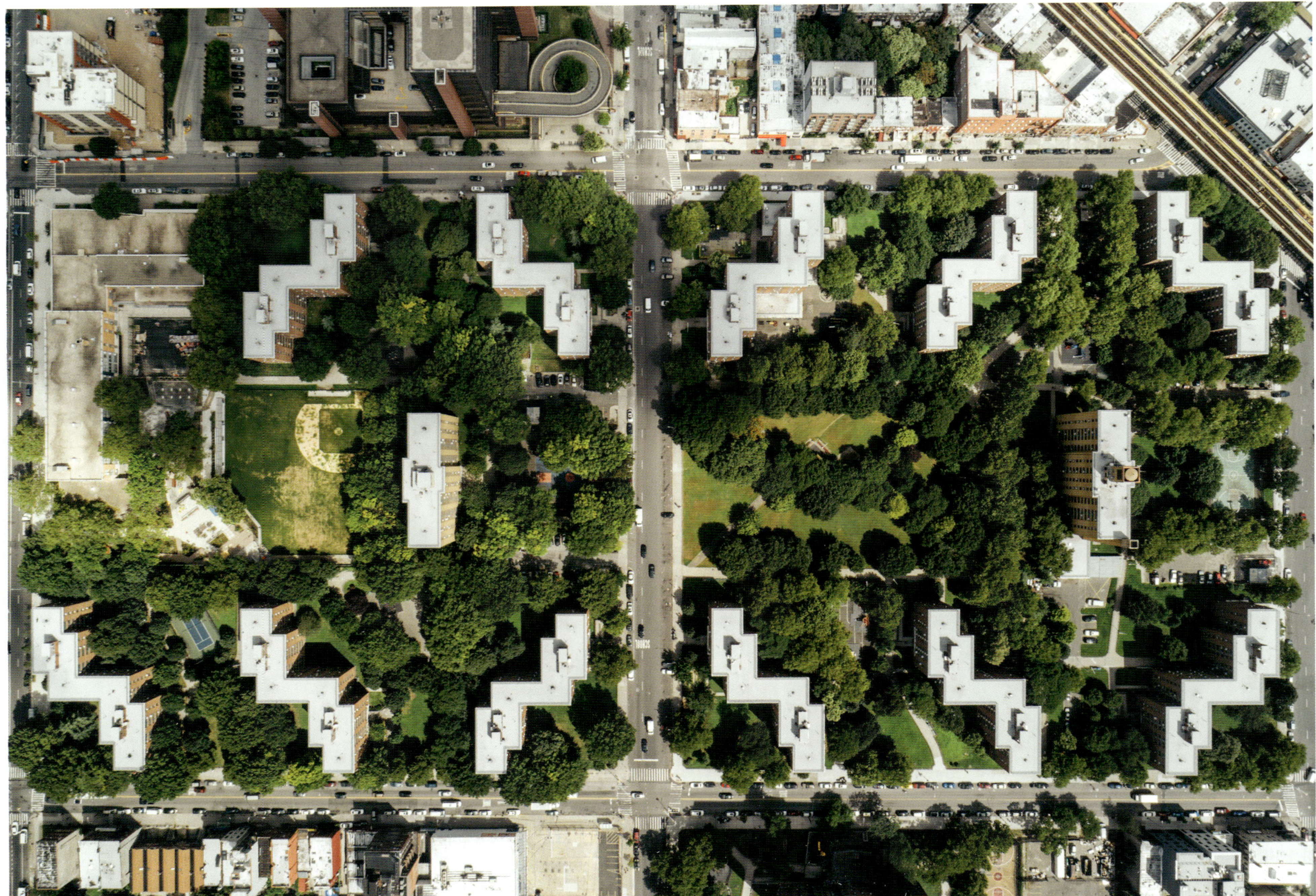

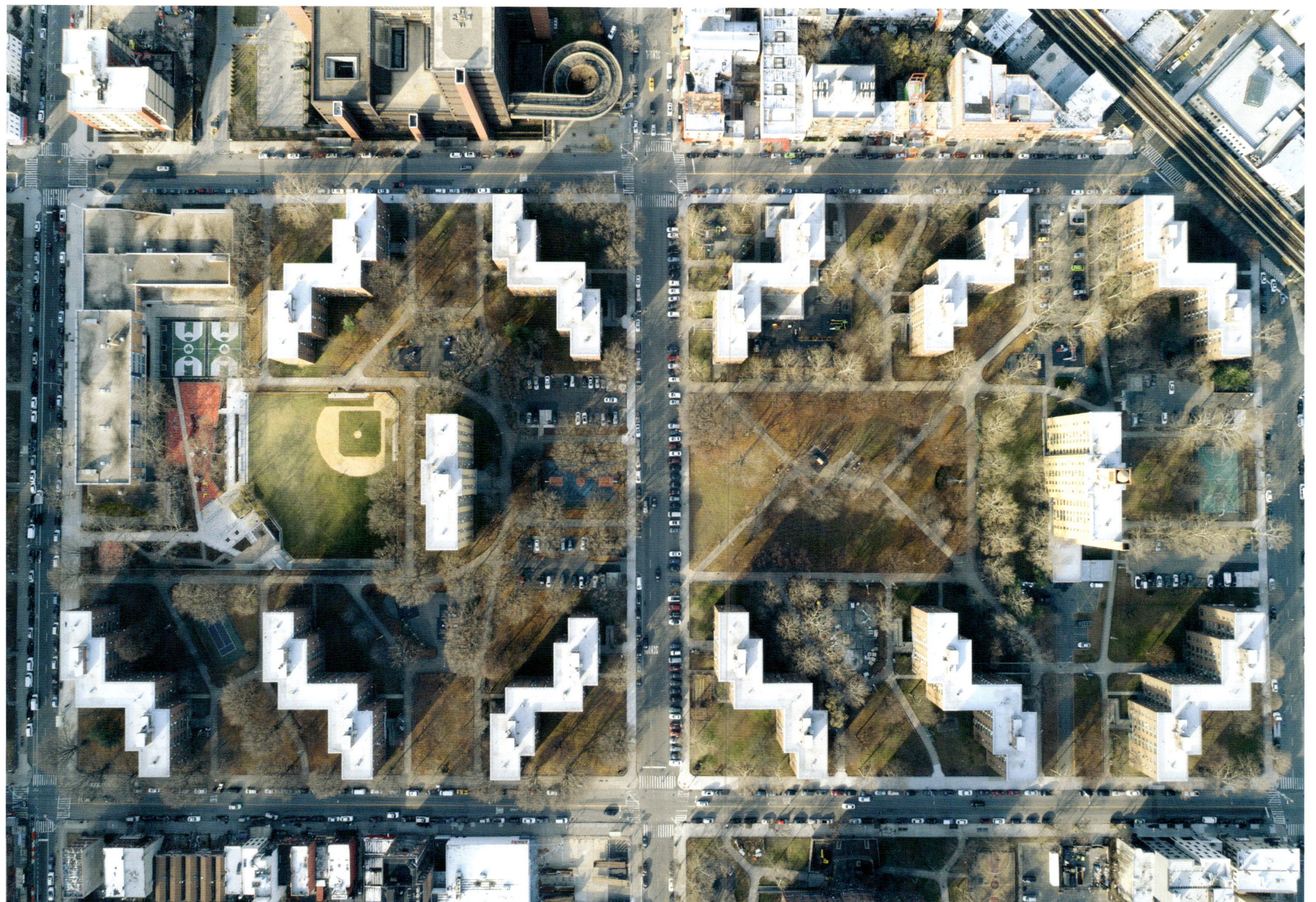

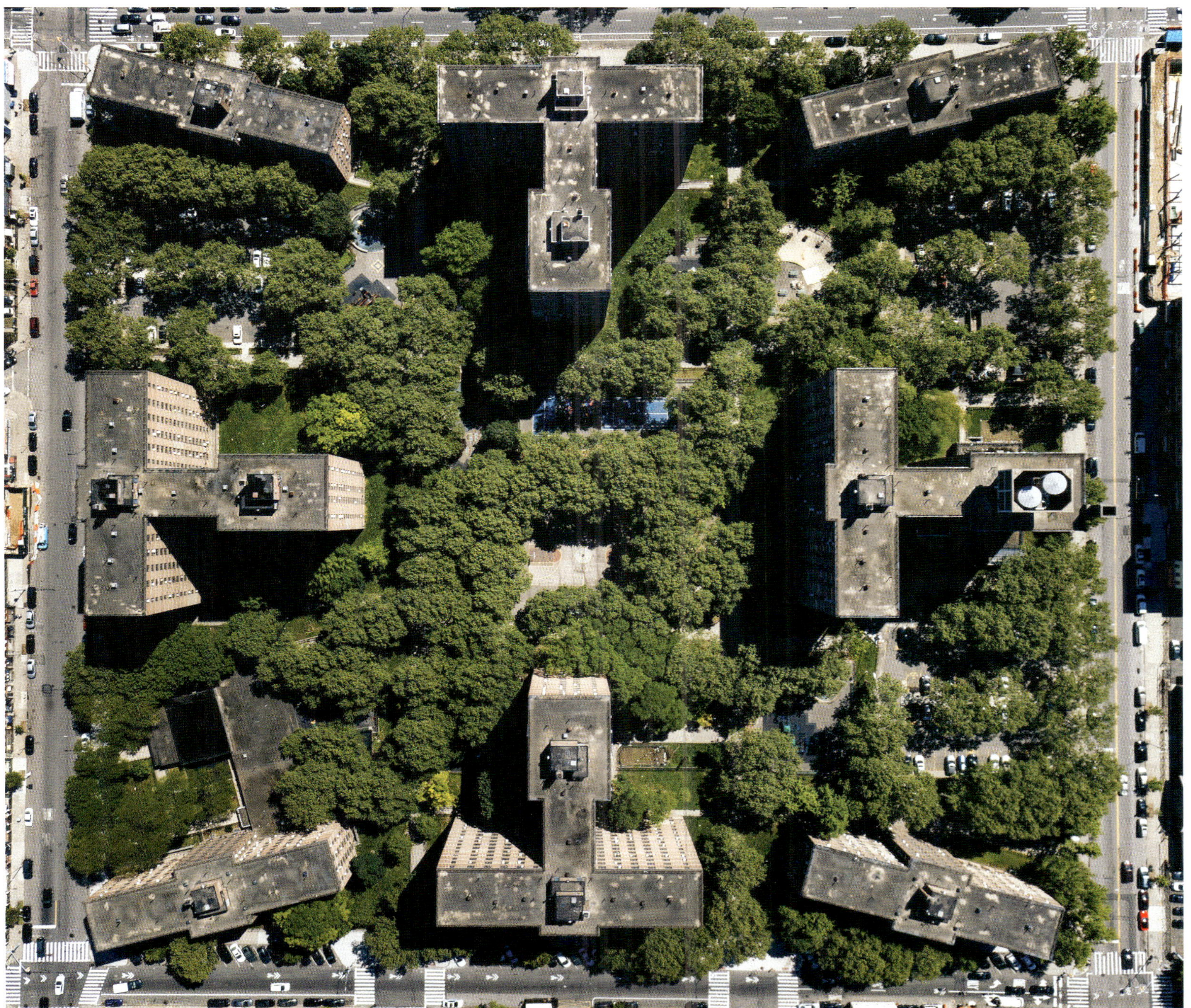

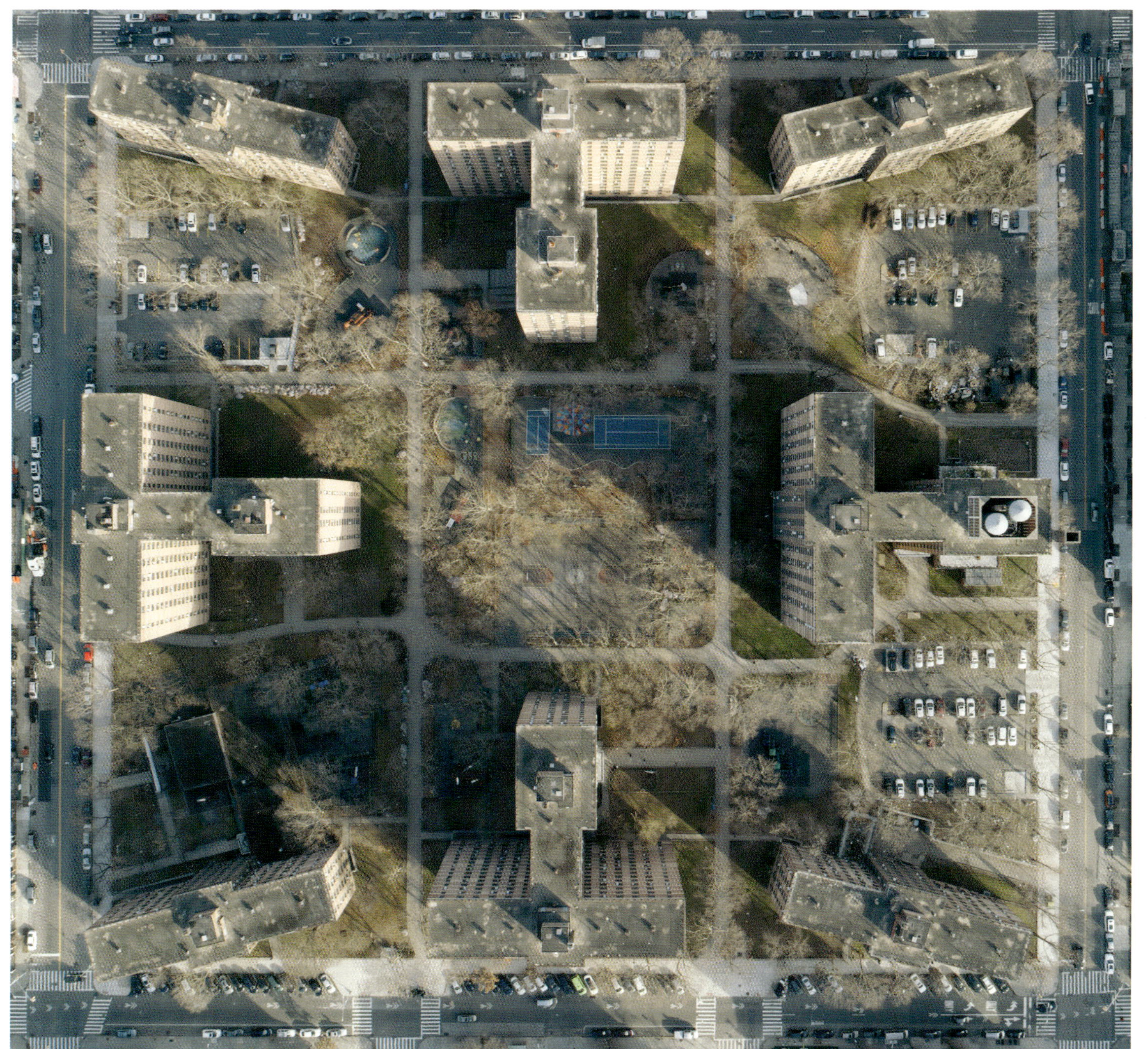

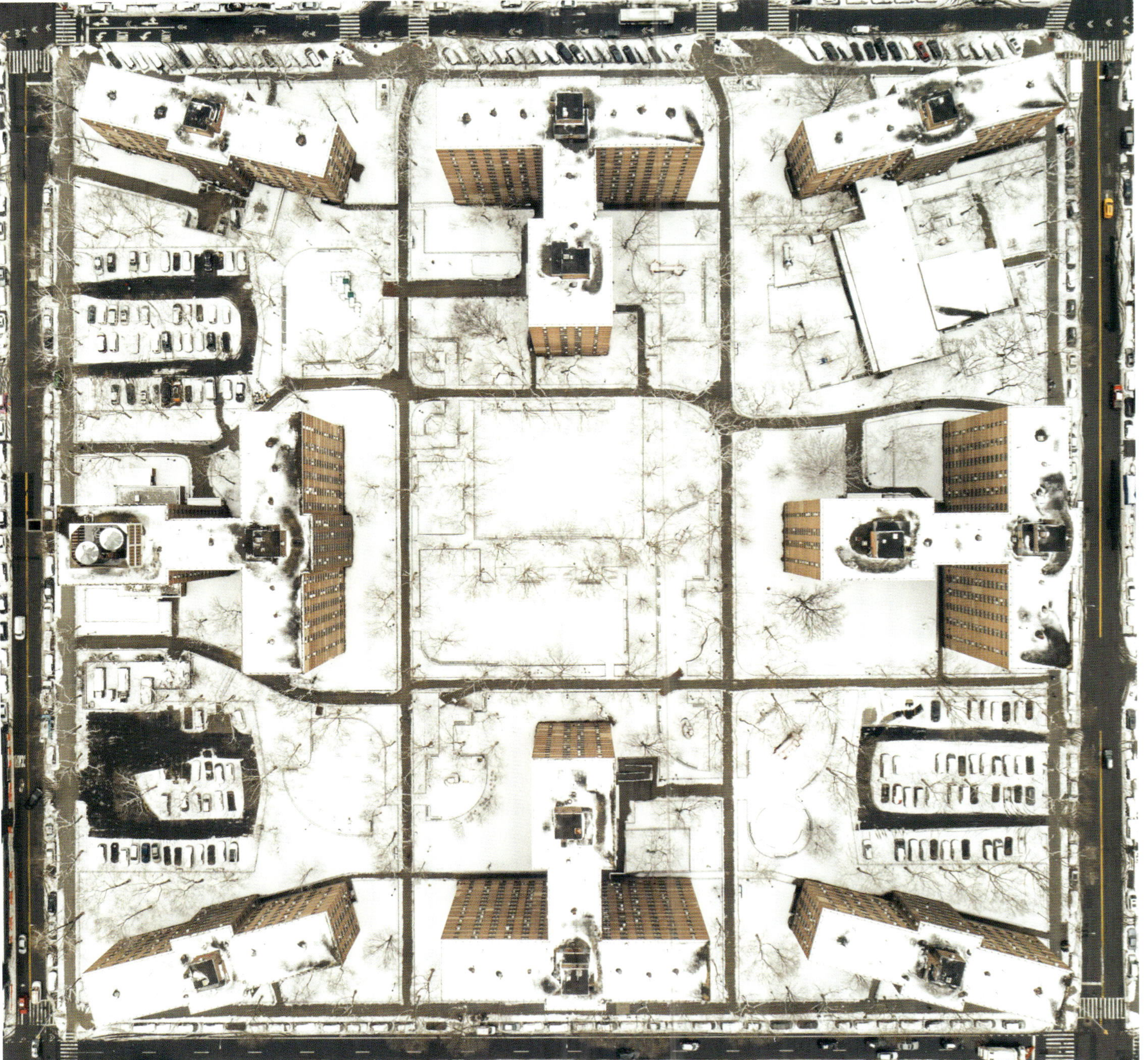

Published by: Gingko Press
in association with BEYOND THE STREETS

All Photography ©Ian Reid

Creative Direction: Roger Gastman

Design & Production: Leon Gonzalez

Writing by Trymaine Lee

Introduction Photo by Cairo Reid

Special Thanks: God, Mom, Cairo,
Trymaine Lee, Jules, Kim Stephens,
Deneice O'Connor, Taylor Bittner, Mobolaji
Dawodu, Sarah, Chioma Nnadi, Gooby,
Skeletor, Spiz, Nick Nick, Rico, BGS,
Clarence N, Kofi, Sacha Jenkins, Roger
Gastman, Aunt Vicky, Leon Gonzalez,
Alyasha Owerka-Moore, Big Lip Phillip,
Kooch, Damany, Amanda Bessette, Just C,
Datwon Thomas, Miss A. Shapiro, Malik
Glover, Rose Erin Vaughn, Don K, Brandon
& Malik—love y'all.

R.I.P to Dad, Karlos, Prince, Celo, LC,
Uncle Junior

Front Cover: Farragut Houses

Back Cover: Pink Houses

Opposite Page: Brownsville Houses

First Edition
0987654321

Printed in Czech Republic

ISBN 978-1-58423-770-9

Gingko Press Inc
2332 4th Street, Suite E
Berkeley, CA 94710

gingkopress.com

beyondthestreets.com

loveian.com

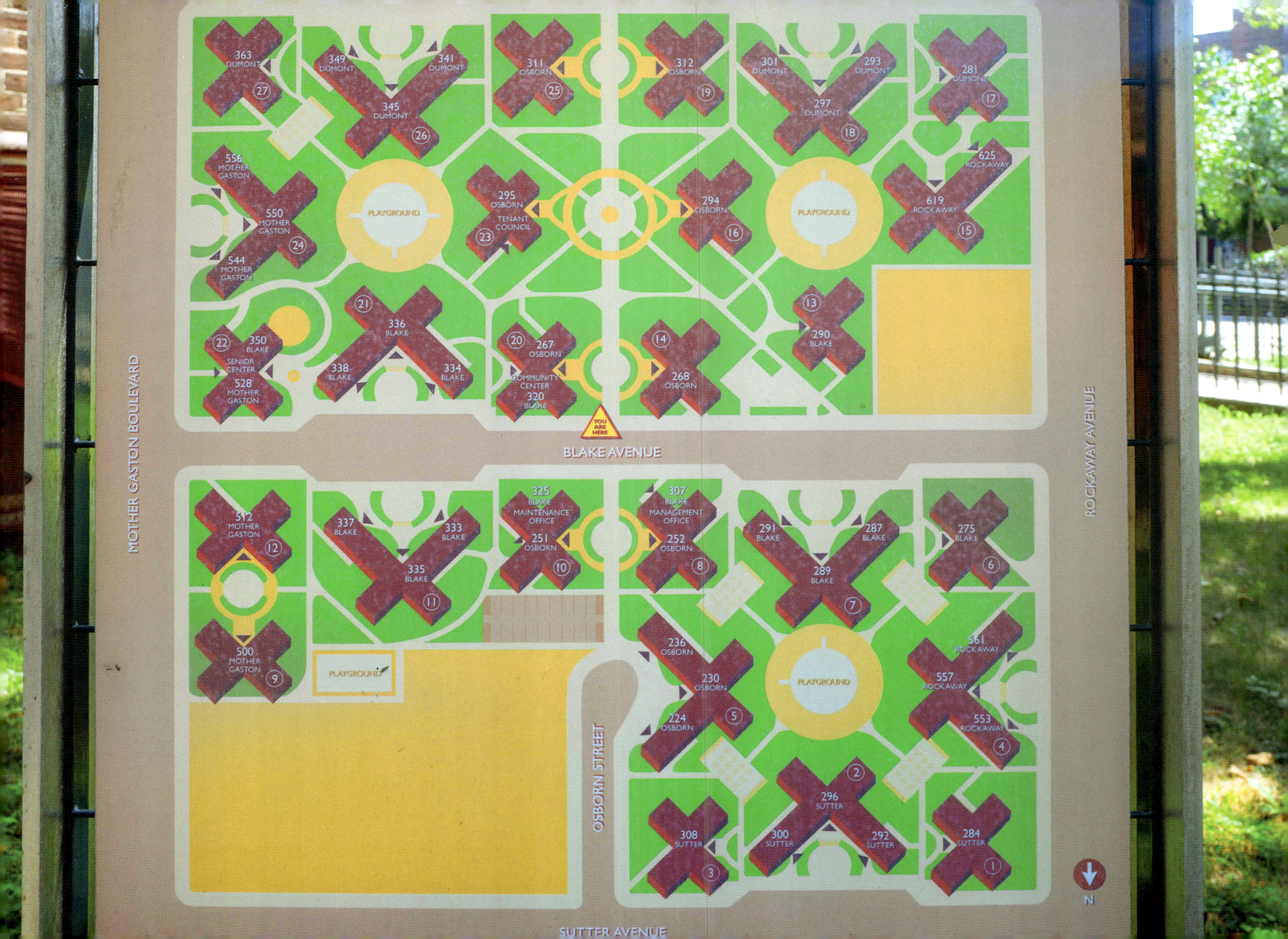

363
DUMONT
27

349
DUMONT

341
DUMONT

311
OSBORN
25

312
OSBORN
19

301
DUMONT

293
DUMONT

281
DUMONT
17

345
DUMONT
26

297
DUMONT
18

625
ROCKAWAY

556
MOTHER
GASTON

550
MOTHER
GASTON
24

295
OSBORN
TENANT
COUNCIL
23

PLAYGROUND

294
OSBORN
16

PLAYGROUND

619
ROCKAWAY
15

544
MOTHER
GASTON

21

336
BLAKE

13

290
BLAKE

22
350
BLAKE
SENIOR
CENTER

528
MOTHER
GASTON

338
BLAKE

334
BLAKE

20
267
OSBORN
COMMUNITY
CENTER
320
BLAKE

14

268
OSBORN

YOU
ARE
HERE

BLAKE AVENUE

512
MOTHER
GASTON
12

337
BLAKE

333
BLAKE

325
BLAKE
MAINTENANCE
OFFICE

251
OSBORN
10

307
BLAKE
MANAGEMENT
OFFICE

252
OSBORN
8

291
BLAKE

287
BLAKE

275
BLAKE
6

335
BLAKE
11

289
BLAKE
7

500
MOTHER
GASTON
9

PLAYGROUND

561
ROCKAWAY

236
OSBORN

557
ROCKAWAY

230
OSBORN

PLAYGROUND

224
OSBORN

5

553
ROCKAWAY

4

2

308
SUTTER

296
SUTTER

300
SUTTER

292
SUTTER

284
SUTTER
1

3

MOTHER GASTON BOULEVARD

ROCKAWAY AVENUE

OSBORN STREET

SUTTER AVENUE

N

...MORE THAN 560,0

RESIDENTS, 1 IN 15,

PUBLIC HOUSING...